P9-BJL-027

"Anything by James K. A. Smith is required reading for Christians wanting to winsomely engage culture. He brings philosophy to the street—putting it to work on the great questions of our time."

Gabe Lyons, Founder, Q Ideas
Author, *The Next Christians*

"Jamie Smith is one of our busiest and most enthusiastic workers—or is it players?—in the vineyards of the Lord. And here we can enjoy a basket of tasty fruits gathered from his daily labors. In these short essays, we see Jamie practicing exactly the sort of wide-ranging Reformed curiosity and engagement that he advocates, sorting out complexities in worship, sport, Christian education, hipster culture, poetry, and more. I'm always grateful for Jamie's work as an astutely critical yet loyal champion of the tradition and a scholar in service of the church. He not only advances the conversation but pushes us to make that conversation matter in the way we live."

Debra Rienstra, Professor of English
Calvin College

"The cultural winds are always blowing, of course, and the difficult challenge is to determine which wind best suits our sails. Jamie Smith's wonderful collection of essays, interviews, letters, and speeches offers a sensible and accessible guide to questions of faith and culture. The pungent stories told here in the frame of allusions to significant contemporary work in the humanities and religious studies provide an invaluable resource for those interested in finding a way forward that sparkles with integrity and hard-won faith. Thankfully, these essays offer respite, hope, and useful instruction to those feeling embattled in the relentlessly changing winds."

Dale Brown, director of the Buechner Institute
King College

"As a busy practitioner leading the church and Christian ministry in this hinge period in history, I often dream of being able to sit down with a discerner of the times—one who both loves the church and understands the intellectual and spiritual subterranean forces that are shaping the way we live and forging the way we live the Christian life. Reading *Discipleship in the Present Tense* is the next best thing to this kind of friendly chat. James K. A. Smith in this delightful assortment of essays, critiques, and interviews is a Christian ethnographer helping the church move through the 'hazy space' between faith and culture, the church and the academy, the historical and the traditional. He does this as a committed scholar in the Reformed tradition, but all of us will find what he says extremely helpful."

Berten A Waggoner, Former National Director
Vineyard USA

"I have learned a lot over the years from James K. A. Smith. I have learned much from these fine essays of his. Every one of them contained many helpful insights. Smith is a pundit, prophet, provocateur, and public intellectual. All these attributes are rolled up together in these fine essays. Whether you are a theologian, philosopher, student, athlete, parent, in a praise band, or just human, Smith's compositions will be of great value to you, just as they are to me."

David Naugle, Professor of Philosophy and
Distinguished University Professor
Dallas Baptist University

Discipleship in the Present Tense

DISCIPLESHIP
IN THE PRESENT TENSE

Reflections on Faith and Culture

JAMES K. A. SMITH

Grand Rapids, Michigan • calvincollegepress.com

Copyright © 2013 by the Calvin College Press

All rights reserved. No part of this publication may be reproduced, stored in a retrieval system, or transmitted, in any form or by any means, electronic, mechanical, photocopying, recording, or otherwise, without the prior written permission of the copyright holder.

Published 2013 by the Calvin College Press
3201 Burton St. SE
Grand Rapids, MI 49546

Printed in the United States of America

Publisher's Cataloging-in-Publication Data
Smith, James K. A., 1970–
Discipleship in the present tense : reflections on faith and culture /
James K. A. Smith.
    p.   cm.
    ISBN 978-1-937555-08-5 (pbk.)
        978-1-937555-09-2 (EPUB)
1. Christian Life. 2. Christian education. 3. Christianity and the
arts. 4. Christianity and culture. 5. Theology. I. Title

BR115.A8 S6 2013   261.5/7—dc23
Library of Congress Control Number: 2013941791

Unless noted, all Scripture quotations are taken from the Holy Bible, New International Version®. NIV®. Copyright © 1973, 1978, 1984 by International Bible Society. All rights reserved worldwide.

Scripture quotations marked NRSV are from the New Revised Standard Version of the Bible, copyright © 1989, by the Division of Christian Education of the National Council of the Churches of Christ in the United States of America. Used by permission. All rights reserved.

Cover design: Robert Alderink and Hyde Creative

For Gary & Barb:
Without their discipleship
these reflections would never
have been possible

CONTENTS

Acknowledgments

A little book like this accrues a disproportionate number of debts. First and foremost, I am indebted to Calvin College for being the unique sort of Christian university that values both advanced, specialized scholarship as well as the important work of "public intellectuals." I'm particularly grateful to work under the care and encouragement of "powers that be" that encourage me to be, well, *me*—to undertake the sort of "translation" work that is represented by the essays in this volume, writing for audiences well beyond the confines of the academic guild. From President Gaylen Byker (and more recently, President Michael Le Roy) to board chairs Bastian Knoppers and Scott Spoelhof to Provost Claudia Beversluis, Deans Cheryl Brandsen and Matt Walhout, and department chairs Del Ratzsch and David Hoekema, I have been tangibly supported and encouraged to devote my energies to the sort of work collected here. I know that is a luxury—and stewardship—and I don't want to take it for granted.

Their support is matched by a gracious network of editors who provide the opportunity and platform for me to "think out loud." As you'll see (each chapter includes indication of its original provenance), most of these essays first received life in magazines like *The Banner, The Other*

Journal, Comment, Perspectives, Christianity Today, and *Harvard Divinity Bulletin.* My wife, Deanna, and I are magazine junkies: we believe in the power of the periodical. Each magazine fosters its own community of conversation, functioning as a sort of parlor that convenes authors and readers in an exchange of ideas. Each has its own slant, its own targets, its own axes to grind, and its own dream to share. As a longtime and voracious reader of magazines, I've always been geeked to contribute to them. (And as the new editor of *Comment* magazine, I'm now eager to curate one.) I'm grateful to all of these editors for permission to reprint the pieces gathered here.

But the work of a public intellectual is a three-legged stool: the first supporting leg is the university; the second is the network of magazines and thought journals that provide a venue; the third leg is that incredible array of sisters and brothers in Christ across a range of vocations and ministries and professions who have invited me into their conversations and have been willing readers. May your tribe increase!

A few more proximate acknowledgments: Thanks to Matt Walhout, editor at the Calvin College Press, for his willingness to support this project and for suggesting an organizing metaphor that gives structure to the book. His advice, coupled with suggestions from Susan Felch, director of the Calvin Center for Christian Scholarship, helped me reconceive the arrangement of the essays that follow. I'm grateful that they've welcomed this book as one of the early volumes to be published by the new Calvin College Press. And I appreciate the support offered by the CCCS in order to make it possible.

The cover image is a photograph that captivated me ever

since I first saw it. It has the additional benefit of having been taken by my daughter, Maddie. Matt Walhout helped me to see it anew as a visual metaphor for this project.

Finally, I'm a grateful to Deanna: for understanding that this kind of writing is what eats up evenings and weekends, and for being so graciously flexible and supportive despite it all.

Living at the Intersection and Reading between the Lines

On Thinking in Public

"What do we do *now*?" This might be the first question of discipleship. It is the question asked by the disciples at the foot of the cross: The Messiah is dead. *What do we do now?* It is the question asked by the same disciples after the resurrection: He's alive! *What do we do now?* And it's the question asked by these Jesus followers after the ascension: The King has left us. *What do we do now?*

While this is the *first* question of discipleship, it is also a *perennial* question of discipleship. If, as Kierkegaard suggests, every generation is contemporaneous with the Messiah—if every follower is a contemporary of the Teacher—then this question will be constantly asked anew. But in order to answer the question, we need to understand this "now"; we need to grapple with the present. So, in a way, "What time is it?" is one of the basic questions for Christian reflection. Christian thought is not an arcane game consumed with systematizing timeless truths; rather, it is a concrete and contemporary task of trying to faithfully discern "the times."

This is why the Christian public intellectual needs to be a kind of ethnographer, offering a "thick description" of our present, attentive to the layers and complexity of those institutions and practices that constitute our contemporary, globalized world. My philosophical work has persistently grappled with the complexities of postmodernity, politics, and public life as a means of trying to understand our present—to discern what time it is, along with the unique challenges, temptations, and pressures that characterize our current context. In the face of these shifting realities, we will often have occasion to ask the disciples' question: What do we do *now*? Christian cultural commentary that is going to offer a thick description of the present needs to be as attentive to "the world" as it is to "the church." Indeed, at times we'll have to complicate the very distinction in order to help the church *be* the church *in* and *for* the world.

So all followers of Jesus—who, on the one hand, are "contemporaries" of Jesus but, on the other hand, inhabit a very different cultural context—all such disciples have to grapple with this question: "What do we do *now*?" The Canadian philosopher Charles Taylor describes ours as a "cross-pressured" situation, one in which we are both pushed and pulled by competing stories and visions of the Good. To be faithful in the present is to be both pressed and stretched, located at the intersection of church and world, past and future, ancient and modern, memory and hope. Christian scholarship that serves the body of Christ is public intellectual labor forged at this intersection.

It is just this sort of intersection that I think is pictured in the image that adorns the cover of this book: a photograph of the Royal Ontario Museum in Toronto, Ontario. This complex structure has become familiar to me, as I get to live in the vicinity of it every summer when I teach at Trinity College at the University of Toronto, just a short stroll down the Philosopher's Walk that curls alongside the ROM. Consider it a visual metaphor for the space in which these chapters were written, a picture of the kind of tension I imagine my readers trying to inhabit. What overwhelms the image is the contemporary, what many of us might experience as the tyranny of the present. So in the foreground is a daunting slice of Daniel Libeskind's remarkable 2007 extension of the museum, known as the Michael Lee-Chin Crystal. It is stark and angular, shiny and modern, recognizably contemporary and self-consciously postmodern, the very embodiment of invention. While it is a structure that some love to hate, I admire its audacity and verve and innovative architectural grammar. It spills onto a sprawling sidewalk and plaza at the corner of Bloor Street and Queen's Park in a way that blurs the line between inside and outside—between the public space of the street and the enclave of the museum. Libeskind wanted this to function as an "open threshold." This in itself is something of a metaphor for the Christian public intellectual, operating in a hazy space between the academy and the church.

But you'll notice a persistent, enduring presence behind Libeskind's creative adventure. The brick and stone building in the background is the Romanesque structure designed by Frank Darling and John A. Pearson as the original home of the museum in 1914. In fact, Libeskind's extension is parasitic upon this historic building, leaning on it while also stretching out from it. Darling and Pearson's design is the architectural memory of the museum, its history and tradition, its heritage. But even when it was built at the turn of the last century, it was already invoking a memory and tradition that was even older. The Romanesque grammar hearkens back to the stones of Venice—and even more immediately, *The Stones of Venice*, John Ruskin's aesthetic and architectural manifesto that spawned a Gothic and Romanesque revival in late 19th-century England (and colonial environs like Ontario). At the heart of that revival was a sense that the ancient was a resource for the contemporary—that the past had wisdom for the present. Ruskin embodied an avant-garde archaicism that found new energy in historic treasures. So when Darling and Pearson were called on to design the *new* Royal Ontario Museum, it's no surprise that they looked to the past, not just for antiquarian interests but as an impetus for artistic creativity that was heir to a tradition of beauty and craftsmanship.

Thank heavens the ROM Board of Governors, at the turn of the 21st century, didn't think they had to choose between heritage and innovation. They didn't decide to raze the Romanesque building to make way for a stand-alone Libeskind creation. No, they commissioned a Libeskind *extension*, recognizing and preserving the integrity of the historical structure. We who visit today inhabit both of these buildings—both of these grammars—simultaneously. We negotiate the different vibes of Libeskind's soaring Crystal and the symmetrical colonnades of the Romanesque structure. We are the ones who need to navigate between tradition and innovation, the historical and the contemporary. A visitor to the Royal Ontario Museum inhabits the intersection between the two.

Again, consider this an architectural metaphor for the Christian life today. We find ourselves in contested spaces, hearing rival gospels, enticed into competing liturgies. Many of us feel a shift in the tectonic plates of plausibility. What's "believable" has changed, and what we have always believed has been challenged. In response to this, some are eager to offer "updated" versions of Christian faith, revisionist versions of the gospel that are more acceptable, less scandalous—more relevant and less offensive. Instead of extending the historic structure, we might say, these proposals envelop it and pretty much flatten it. I suggest a different strategy, one that looks to the resources of the tradition as a way forward.

We are heirs of "the faith that was once for all entrusted to the saints" (Jude 3) but also enjoined to "become all things to all people, that [we] might by all means save some" (1 Cor. 9:22 NRSV). In my corner of the body of Christ, this intersection is captured in something of a motto: we are Reform*ed*, but always reform*ing*. Nothing is simply settled; but neither is everything up for grabs. Faithfulness requires knowing the difference between authentic extensions versus assimilative adaptations. To follow Jesus today—and to be the body of Christ today—cannot be reduced to simply parroting what we've said and done in the past. We inhabit a different time. The answer to the question "What time is it?" has changed. And so faithfulness requires innovation and cultural agility. At the same time, we are called to be the one people of God, enduring over time, serving the One who is the same yesterday, today, and forever. So faithfulness also requires fidelity and a grateful reception of the wisdom of the tradition. This is why the temporal question—"What time is it?"—is a necessarily prelude to the discipleship question—"What do we do *now*?" And the resources for answering that question are ancient.

What you'll find in this book is a collection of essays that, I hope, try to answer both questions. These essays are written at a number of different intersections: at the intersection of faith and culture; at the intersection of the historic Christian tradition and the pressing challenges of the present; at the intersection of church and academy; even at the intersection of faith and doubt. The chapters that follow address a range of themes and topics that include parenting and politics, poetry and praise bands, pedagogy and painting, and much more—areas of life that are themselves complex tangles of competing trajectories.

What all of the essays share in common is the conviction that Christian scholars are called to help the body of Christ live faithfully at these intersections. This isn't a conviction that is ever made explicit *in* them; rather, it is a conviction that is performed *by* these essays. They are the enactment of my sense of obligation to the church as that "public" which the Christian scholar is called to serve. Christian scholars in various disciplines are uniquely equipped to discern the shape of our present, to answer the question "What time is it?" Indeed, we might think of the Christian university as something of a think tank for the church, wherein the body of Christ commissions a community of scholars to put their scholarly gifts and training to work for the sake of discipleship (though not *only* for that). Conversely, Christian scholars—especially those at Christian colleges and universities—are recipients of a trust and a commission. As such, we should be looking for opportunities to be stewards of our academic training in ways that can contribute to the maturity and growth of the body of Christ (Eph. 4:11–16), even when such thinking demands critique and challenge.

This is what I describe as outreach scholarship: scholarship *for* practice, Christian scholarship for the church. Such work is very different from specialized scholarship for our respective academic guilds, in several different ways. The work of a Christian public intellectual is necessarily *occasional*: it is in response to realities and challenges on the ground, which change not only over time but, increasingly, over the course of a 24-hour news cycle. So some of the essays included here are responding to a particular context at a particular time. Nonetheless, I include them in this book both because the issues involved often transcend the particular occasion and because there might be lessons in how to engage other issues on other occasions.

Such writing is also inherently *interdisciplinary*: the messy complexity of "real world" questions refuses to be neatly carved up into the specialized silos of academic disciplines, which is why the Christian public intellectual always risks traipsing on someone else's turf (and suffering the wrath of a thousand specialist qualifications as a result). Furthermore, such writing is a mix of analysis and prescription, summary and discernment. One could say that part of the task is to help the body of Christ find the lines of intersection, define the points of tension, discern the trajectories of implication, and chart a course for faithful practice going forward. The Christian scholar should help his sisters and brothers to answer the question "What time is it?" *so that* he can then come alongside them to ask, "What should we do *now*?" With respect to the former question, the Christian scholar speaks with the authority of her or his disciplinary training. But with respect to the latter sort of question, the playing field is leveled, and the scholar comes alongside the community of faith as we together, led by the Spirit, try to discern a faithful way forward.

But perhaps above all, I think such writing has to be *charitable*, even when it is forthrightly critical and polemical. The work of the Christian public intellectual should be motivated by love for God and neighbor, finding expression in a deep desire to help the body of Christ embody the gospel faithfully. Only such love can sustain the energy needed to do this work of translation. And only charity can help the scholar navigate the intersection between the academy and the church. Without it, we are prone to lapse into the condescension that is too often cultivated by the institutions that train us. Readers can quickly and easily sense the difference between a critique that is dismissive and condescending versus a critique that is animated by a deep love for the church.

Finally, as a Christian scholar who is a philosopher and theologian, I consider myself an heir and steward of the riches of the Christian tradition, a guardian and defender of ancient treasures in our contemporary moment. Everything in this book is animated by the conviction that the tradition of Christian orthodoxy is a gift, not a liability—a resource for the future, not an embarrassment that we should be trying to sweep under the carpet or tuck away in a back room like a crazy uncle. Following Robert Webber's notion of an "ancient-future" faith, I see a 5th-century bishop like Saint

Augustine as a 21st-century sage. I look to a 16th-century Reformer like John Calvin as an ally in trying to discern the shape of faith culture-making in our new millennium. So while these essays try to take seriously the unique dynamics of our present, they do so with a long view, encouraging contemporary Christians to find buried treasure in the heritage that is already ours. To live at that intersection is to be caught up in the life of our incarnating God, who at the fullness of time intersected with history and now invites us, ever anew, to be his contemporaries.

Part 1

STORY LINES
Outlines of the Reformed Tradition

EVERY GENERATION NEEDS TO TELL THE STORY ANEW—
to rehearse the narrative of God's gracious redemption and find words for the hope within us. This impetus to tell and re-tell is as old as God's covenant with Israel (Deut. 6:4-15). Every re-telling is a telling anew, in a new context, at a new time, at a new intersection of challenges and cross-pressures. But re-telling is not the same as merely repeating.

The essays in this section are examples of such retellings, rehearsing familiar story lines in a new context. Each of these chapters revisits core convictions of the Christian faith, often with a Reformed accent, in order to rearticulate them for a new time and audience. The goal is to refresh our appreciation for themes we might come to take for granted (or worse, given that familiarity tends to breed contempt). So I take it to be a virtue of these chapters that they don't really say anything new! On the other hand, I do hope that they articulate historic convictions *anew*—in ways that put "traditional" convictions in a new light, granting them fresh rationales. In this sense, they work differently for different readers: if these themes are new to you, then I hope they'll function as invitations to fresh, hitherto unappreciated aspects of Christian wisdom; if they are familiar to you, I hope they'll rekindle your appreciation and affirmation of their importance—and perhaps dissuade you from abandoning them just because they're "traditional." Familiarity is not a sufficient criterion for abandonment.

Finally, you'll note that the essays in this section especially home in on themes and convictions that are central to the Reformed tradition of which I am a part. I don't want to pretend to write from nowhere, as if it were possible to be "generically" Christian. Instead, I write unapologetically as a catholic Christian—situated in the historic faith of Augustine and Aquinas, Erasmus and Luther, Jonathan Edwards and Pope Benedict XVI—but I do so with a distinct Reformed *accent*. In fact, I think the best way to be "Catholic" is to be unapologetically parochial—to be catholic *from somewhere*. This is a concrete, embodied place to stand, and from which I try to discern the lines of historic Christian faith for a postmodern age.

REDEMPTION

As Big as Creation, Far as the Curse Is Found

What love is this that would take such risks? The covenant God of Israel and Father of Jesus Christ is an extravagant, fecund Creator who—in what almost looks like madness— entrusted the care and unpacking of creation to us, his creatures, commissioned as his image bearers. Deputized and gifted to carry out this mission of image-bearing cultivation, God enjoins us to get to work and go play, to make love and art, to till the earth and transform its fruit into our daily bread while also inventing the most outlandish dreams in cathedrals and skyscrapers. Such image-bearing culture-making will be most fruitful when it runs with the grain of the universe—when our work and play run with the grooves of God's life-giving norms.

Creation, then, comes with a mission and a vocation. Being God's image bearers is a task and responsibility entrusted to creatures. If God created from and for love, then

---

"Redemption," *Comment* (Spring 2010): 14–17. Reprinted with permission.

he also created us with the invitation to love the world and thus foster its—and *our*—flourishing.

But . . .

We confess—and all too often experience—a rupture in this vision for a carnival of creative love. God's self-giving love entrusted to us the care and cultivation of his creation, but humanity seized this as an entitlement rather than receiving it as a gift. Thus our mission of unfolding the potential latent in creation took the form of unfettered invention rather than normed cocreation. While this creational impulse for *poiēsis* could not be effaced or erased, this good creational impulsion to *make* became twisted and misdirected: instead of making love, we made war (and now even when we make love we are prone to do so in ways that run counter to what's actually good for us). Instead of cultivating the earth, we've created entire systems that rapaciously despoil it. Instead of normed making, humanity is prone to licentious breaking. We have failed to carry out the mission entrusted to us as God's image bearers.

And Yet . . .

Our good Creator has not left us to our own devices. Although we ruptured the plenitude of creative love, our condescending God has ruptured our brass heaven, overwhelming our desire to enclose ourselves in immanence by appearing in the flesh—*our* flesh—as the image of the invisible God. Jesus of Nazareth appears as the second Adam, who models for us what it looks like to carry out that original mission of image bearing and cultivation. The Word became flesh not to save our souls *from* this fallen world, but in order to restore us as lovers *of* this world—to (re)enable us to carry out that creative commission. Indeed, God saves us so that—once again, in a kind of divine madness—we, as an empowered, Spirit-filled people, can save the world, can (re)make the world aright. And God's redemptive love spills over in its cosmic effects, giving hope to this groaning creation.

So our redemption is not some supplement to being human; it's what makes it possible to be *really* human, to take up the mission that marks us as God's image bearers. Saint Irenaeus captures this succinctly: "The glory of God is a human being fully alive." Redemption doesn't tack on some spiritual appendage, nor does it liberate us from being human in order to achieve some sort of angelhood. Rather, redemption is the restoration of our humanity, and our humanity is bound up with our mission of being God's cocreative culture-makers. While God's redemption is cosmic, not anthropocentric, it nonetheless operates according to that original creational scandal whereby humans are commissioned as ambassadors, and even cocreators, for the sake of the world. In an equally scandalous way, we are now commissioned as coredeemers. Redemption is the reorientation and redirection of our culture-making capacities. It is we who have invented the twisted cultural systems that deface and despoil this good world; restoring creation to its lush plenitude and fecundity will not happen by divine fiat or magic—it will require the hard, patient, Spirit-inspired work of building well-ordered systems, creation-caring institutions, and life-giving habits. While not quite a matter of "save the cheerleader, save the world," the scandalous economy of redemption does seem to suggest, "save humanity, save the world."

One of the New Testament words for "salvation" (*sotēria*) carries the connotations of both deliverance and liberation as well as health and well-being. So salvation is both liberation from our disorder and the restoration of health and flourishing. I can think of no better picture of this than the sort of health-giving practices that Wendell Berry notices and celebrates in his recent collection *Bringing It to the Table: On Farming and Food*. Consider, for example, his praise of Amish farmers in northeastern Indiana who are "working to restore farmed-out soils." That is a compact rendition of our redemptive calling. Systems, institutions, and practices have grown up that fail to care for the soil (and the animals who live from it); they leech it and steal from it without restoring it. The error, yea sin, of such ill-gotten gain will show itself soon enough because such systems and practices run against the grain of the universe. Creation itself tells us what we're doing wrong. Redemption, in this case, is tangible and concrete: it's rotating crops, spreading manure, and being attuned to what the soil is telling us. Working to restore farmed-out soils is situated within a way of life—indeed *is* a way of life.

Thanks be to God, such redeeming, health-giving, cultural labor is not the special province of Christians. While the church is that people who have been regenerated and empowered by the Spirit to do the good work of culture-making, foretastes of the coming, flourishing kingdom are not confined to the church. The Spirit is profligate in spreading seeds of hope. So we gobble up foretastes of the kingdom wherever we can find them. The creating, redeeming God of Scripture takes delight in Jewish literature that taps the deep recesses of language's potential, in Muslim commerce that runs with the grain of the universe, and in the well-ordered marriages of agnostics and atheists. We, too, can follow God's lead and celebrate the same.

But what does redemption look like? For the most part, you'll know it when you see it, because it looks like flourishing. It looks like a life well lived. It looks like the way things are supposed to be. It looks like a well-cultivated orchard laden with fruit produced by ancient roots. It looks like labor that builds the soul and brings delight. It looks like an aged husband and wife laughing uproariously with their great-grandchildren. It looks like a dancer stretching her body to its limit, embodying a stunning beauty in muscles and sinews rippling with devotion. It looks like the graduate student hunched over a microscope, exploring nooks and crannies of God's microcreation, looking for ways to undo the curse. It looks like abundance for all.

All of this will look like grace if and only if you have a deep sense of the corrupting, disordering, cosmic effects of sin. Only if you appreciate the radical effects of the Fall can you begin to literally see the grace of what look like everyday realities.

So redemption can sound like the surprising cadences of a Bach concerto whose rhythm seems to expand the soul. It sounds like an office that hums with a sense of harmony in mission, punctuated by collaborative laughter. It sounds like the grunts and cries of a tennis player whose blistering serve and liquid forehand are enactments of things we couldn't have dreamed possible. It sounds like the questions of a third-grader whose teacher loves her enough to elicit and make room for a sanctified curiosity about God's good world. It even sounds like the spirited argument of a young couple who are discerning just what it means for their marriage to be a friendship that pictures the community God desires (and is).

Redemption smells like the oaky tease of a Napa Chardonnay that births anticipation in our taste buds. It smells like soil under our nails after laboring over peonies and gerber daisies. It smells like the steamy winter kitchen of a family together preparing for supper. It smells like the ancient wisdom of a book inherited from a grandfather, or that "outside smell" of the family dog in November. It smells like riding your bike to work on a foggy spring morning. It even smells like the salty pungence of hard work or that singular bouquet of odors that bathes the birth of a child.

Redemption tastes like a fall harvest yielded though loving labor and attentive care for soil and plant. It tastes like a Thanksgiving turkey whose very "turkeyness" comes to life from its own animal delight on a free range. It tastes like the delightful hoppy bitterness of an IPA shared with friends at the neighborhood pub. It even tastes like eating your broccoli because your mother loves you enough to want you to eat well.

So redemption looks like the bodily poetry of Rafael Nadal and the boyish grin of Brett Favre on a good night; it sounds like the amorous giggles of Julia and Paul Child and smells like her kitchen; it reverberates like the deep anthems of Yo-Yo Ma's cello; it feels like the trembling meter of Auden's poetry or the spry delight of Updike's light verse; it looks like the compassionate care of Paul Farmer and Mother Theresa. Redemption can be spectacular and fabulous and (almost) triumphant.

But for the most part, Spirit-empowered redemption looks like what Raymond Carver calls "a small, good thing." It looks like our everyday work done well, out of love, in resonance with God's desire for his creation—so long as our on-the-ground labor is nested as part of a contribution to systems and structures of flourishing. It looks like doing our homework, making the kids' lunches for school, building with quality and a craftsman's devotion, and crafting a municipal budget that discerns what really matters and contributes to the common good. Of course, redemption is the fall of apartheid, but it's also the once-impossible friendships forged in its aftermath. It's an open seat on the bus for everyone, but it's also getting to know my neighbors who differ from me. It's nothing short of trying to change the world, but it starts in our homes, our churches, our neighborhoods, and our schools.

It should not surprise us that redemption will not always look triumphant. If Jesus comes as the second Adam, who models redemptive culture-making, then in our broken world such cultural labor will look cruciform. But it will also look like hope that is hungry for joy and delight.

2

Buried Treasures

On the Riches of the Reformed Tradition

Imagine that you've been invited to the home of a new friend. You've driven by their house a few times before and noticed that it's a gorgeous arts and crafts masterpiece—an exquisite piece of craftsmanship, dripping with the sort of quality and heritage you can no longer find in a pragmatic world concerned only with the bottom line.

Based on what you know, you expect to be ushered into

"Buried Treasures?," *The Banner* 146, no. 1 (January 2011): 32–35. Reprinted with permission. This essay began its life as a talk for the Board of the Trustees for my denomination, The Christian Reformed Church of North America (www.crcna.org), along with the boards of our denominational agencies including Faith Alive, the denominational publishing agency mentioned below. Often abbreviated as the CRC, this is a historic Reformed denomination with Dutch roots that subscribes to the Reformed confessions like the Belgic Confession and the Heidelberg Catechism. In addition, the CRC issued a "contemporary testimony" in 1986 entitled *Our World Belongs to God* (see www.crcna.org/welcome/beliefs/contemporary-testimony/our-world-belongs-god). This testimony, like the denomination that produced it, is uniquely influenced by the Dutch journalist, statesman, and theologian Abraham Kuyper (1837–1920).

an interior lifted right out of a Frank Lloyd Wright museum—a foyer ushering you into a parlor lush with warm wooden trim and the elegant simplicity of mission cabinets in dark oak finishes, with Morris & Co. wallpaper hand-blocked on cloth and floors covered with sumptuous hand-woven carpets. You'll make your way into the dining room to see the ancient handcraft of custom glass, and then you'll proceed into an elegant, classic kitchen. In short, you're eager to visit the house because, if you're like me, it seems to promise everything you love about architecture and design. You're expecting a house that stands out precisely because of its anachronism, its connection to tradition—traditions of craftsmanship, quality, and design that have been lost in a culture more driven by pragmatism, speed, and the bottom line.

Expecting something like that, imagine your surprise when, entering the house, you find something starkly different. A garish linoleum covers the precious tile that you just *know* is under the entryway. Dropped ceilings have shut down the transcendent space of what would have been 10-foot ceilings. At some point in the '70s someone decided that orange Astroturf was better than classic hardwood. Then at some point in the '80s someone must have surmised that tacky mirrors were more contemporary than stained glass. And as you make your way into the kitchen, you notice that someone in the '60s, armed with pea-green plastic, thought they could improve upon the ancient craftsmanship of the house you just know is dying to breathe underneath all of this renovation. And you find yourself reeling from the cognitive dissonance between what you were expecting on the outside and what you find on the inside.

Finding Hidden Treasure

I offer this as a bit of an allegory. But it will make more sense if I share a little bit of my testimony. As you might have guessed from the my last name, I was not raised in the CRC. I am a convert to a Reformed world-and-life view, a pilgrim who has made his way to the Reformed tradition, and the CRC in particular, as my confessional and ecclesiastical (and intellectual) home.

I was a relatively late convert to Christian faith, having been raised in non-Christian home. I came to Christ through a sector of Christendom that was on the more fundamentalist end of evangelicalism. But in my sophomore year at college, I made my first discovery of the Reformed tradition: in older voices like Calvin and Warfield, but also in more contemporary voices like Francis Schaeffer and Alvin Plantinga. For me, this was like finding buried treasure. This began a pilgrimage—both spiritual and intellectual—that would later lead me to membership in the CRC.

What was it that attracted me to the Reformed tradition? It was not any *one* thing. Instead, it was a kind of seamless cloth of related emphases that, I think, are the unique "apostolate" of the Reformed tradition, and the CRC in particular. That is, the CRC is a unique expression of the Reformed tradition that tends to hold together an array of gifts that in other places are separated. In particular, I would highlight four distinctives in this regard:

1. A celebration of a covenant-keeping Lord. Central to the Reformed tradition is both a unique emphasis on the unity of the narrative of Scripture and a strong sense of our *communal* identity as "a people." There is an entire theology packed into the pronouns of Scriptures. From that opening "us" of the creational word in Genesis 1:26 ("Let us make humanity in our image"), to the "them" of Genesis 1:27 ("male and female he created them"), to the plural "you" of the creational mandate in Genesis 1:29 ("I give you every seed-bearing plant"), God's creation is laden with plurals! (It's also a little tough to "be fruitful and multiply" all by yourself, if you know what I mean). And all of those "yous" in the Bible are also in the plural. Those of us formed by the individualism of North American culture tend to read those "yous" as if the Bible was sort of privately addressed to *me*— as if the "you" was singular. But I think our indigenous and Korean brothers and sisters hear the Scriptures more clearly on these matters: the "you" is *us*. It's not *me*, but *we*. It is just this sort of communal emphasis that is highlighted by the Reformed tradition's covenant theology, which is also why it yields a holistic, unified reading of the canon of Scripture as the one unfolding story of God's covenant with his people.

2. An affirmation of the goodness of creation. Contrary to the dualism and functional Gnosticism of wider evangelicalism, the unique emphasis on the goodness of creation— a theme we inherit especially from Abraham Kuyper and his heirs—is one of the real gems in the Reformed treasure chest, and one that distinguishes the CRC's heritage from other, more narrow versions of Reformed theology.

3. An exhortation to "make culture" *well.* Growing out of that affirmation of the goodness of creation, the Reformed tradition values good work as an expression of God's calling. But it also is discerning and knows that God desires culture and institutions made for the flourishing of creation. And so it is precisely an emphasis on culture that informs our concerns about *justice*: think of the laments in *Our World Belongs to God*, which recognize the range of ways that God wants to delight us, but also the plethora of ways that we've fallen short, creating institutions and practices that run counter to the grain of the universe.

4. A connection to our catholic heritage. This might seem a little strange, but for me, becoming Reformed was a way of becoming catholic. What do I mean by that? The Reformers were not revolutionaries; that is, they were not out to raze the church to the ground, get back to some pure set of New Testament church principles, and start from scratch. In short, they didn't see themselves as leapfrogging over the centuries of post-apostolic tradition. They were *re-form*ing the church. And in that respect, they saw themselves as heirs and debtors to the tradition that had come before them. Indeed, they understood the Spirit as unfolding the wisdom of the Word over the centuries in the voices of Augustine and Gregory the Great, of Chrysostom and Anselm. To say the Reformed tradition is catholic is just to say that it affirms this operation of the Spirit *in history* and thus receives the gifts of tradition as gifts of the Spirit, subject to the Word. This is inscribed in the very heart of the Heidelberg Catechism, which explicates the Christian faith by unpacking the Apostles' Creed—a heritage of the church catholic.

Let me unpack this last point just a little more: what I mean to emphasize is that the Reformed tradition is not just a set of doctrines; nor is it just a unique worldview; it is also a unique nexus of practices, including worship, that represent the accrued wisdom of the church led by the Spirit. (A wonderful, compact summary of this can be found in the prologue to Faith Alive's *Worship Sourcebook*.) Worship is where we meet God, and worship is how we are formed by the Spirit into the people of God. So how we worship is an intentional, embodied, received expression of what it means to be Reformed—and the shape of that worship is a gift from the "catholic" heritage of Spirit at work in history.

It is this unique web of distinctives that has made the CRC produce such a unique configuration of ministries and agencies, the fruit of this interrelated web of Reformed themes that are often rent asunder in other traditions.

Buried?

It was these themes—covenant, creation, culture, and catholicity—that drew me to the Reformed tradition. And I was always a little surprised to learn that there was one denomination that held all of these things together—no mean feat! Discovering these was like discovering buried treasure. And there are Christians and new converts all over the world who are finding these gifts of the Reformed tradition to be a new, deeper spirituality that conforms them to the image of Christ. When folks like me discover the Reformed tradition, we ask in amazement: Where have you *been* all my life?

But permit me one observation. As someone who looks on these Reformed themes as an incredible gift of the Spirit, as new riches, as welcome nourishment compared with the spiritual impoverishment I knew before, I've been puzzled as to why so many CRC congregations, institutions, and agencies seem almost eager to paper over some of them.

As a pilgrim and convert to the Reformed tradition in all its fullness, I came running to the CRC expecting to find inside all the riches of an arts and crafts masterpiece. Instead, I have to say that often enough I've found something more like the garish orange living room—something that aims to be an "updated" version of the faith covering up the riches underneath.

Now, I think I understand why this might be: Some have been rightly concerned that what was often valued as "Reformed" was really just "Dutch." And they rightly understand that the proclamation of God's kingdom, and an invitation into the people of God, is not a matter of taking on the particularities of some ethnic heritage. And so we have spent a generation sifting the tradition, as it were, in order to sift out the dross of an ethnic heritage from the treasures of the Spirit.

That is an important, crucial concern—and just right. But I worry that something else has happened along the way: that we have inadvertently fallen into the trap of thinking that Reformed Christian faith is a kind of content or message that can be distilled and then dropped into other so-called "relevant" or "contemporary" containers. But the Christian faith—and the Reformers understood this—is not just a set of doctrines or beliefs, a know-*what* "message" that we come to believe. Christian faith is also a kind of know-*how* into which we are apprenticed. It is an understanding of the world that we absorb through practice. And that understanding is embedded in the received practices of Reformed worship, which is precisely why the Reformers were so concerned about the shape of worship. They did not think worship was just a pragmatic matter of getting people's attention and disseminating a message. Worship is a formative encounter with a living, active, covenant-keeping Lord. And the Reformers appreciated that we are indebted to the accrued wisdom of the church that, led by the Spirit, discerned certain nonnegotiable elements of the *form* of worship that carries all of these distinctives of Reformed Christian faith. We are what we worship; we are also *how* we worship.

So if we're considering the future of the CRC and the nature of Reformed identity, we might do well to ask ourselves some uncomfortable questions:

- Have we papered over the riches of our Reformed heritage?
- In our desire to be relevant, have we buried the treasures of Reformed identity?
- In our quest to be contemporary, have we overlooked the missional resources in Reformed particularity?
- In sifting the dross of an ethnic heritage, have we tossed out the treasures of the Spirit?

A Reformed Future

I worry that in trying to update the Reformed tradition, in trying to be contemporary and relevant, we've sometimes abandoned the historic wisdom of the tradition. Sometimes we've done this because we think this is the future of the CRC—that if the CRC is going to survive, we need to get with it and start looking more like others. But that, my friends, is to bury exactly the riches we have—and the riches that others are looking for. If the CRC wants to just become generic evangelicalism, or bland Protestant liberalism, then there's really no reason for us to exist. There are others already doing that.

But I want to testify that there are people all over the world who are hungry for the treasures that sometimes seem to embarrass us. There are Christians in Indonesia and Nigeria, Vancouver and San Francisco, who are hungry for what we take for granted. There are young people all over the world who don't yet know Christ who will be drawn to him, not by another "event" that looks like the concert or club they went to last weekend, but by the strange transcendence of Reformed worship in all its unapologetic fullness— and who will see that these are the practices of a people concerned with justice and flourishing *in this world*, too.

I fear we spend a lot of energy trying to figure out how to be like others when others are actually jealous of what we already have. I only want to suggest to you that the richest future for the CRC might be in remembering the riches of our heritage—sifted and refined, to be sure. But with that discernment, I want to provocatively suggest that the future of being Reformed might be catholic. Our future is most hopeful, I think, when we think of it as an intentional, careful *restoration* project rather than a merely updating renovation.

3

A Peculiar People?

Between Places

I recently returned to Canada for a two-week sojourn to teach at the University of Toronto. This was a homecoming of sorts—to my "home and native land," to the familiar environs of the U of T, and to the vicinity of the Institute for Christian Studies where I did my master's degree. But as I was strolling around Queen's Park one evening, contemplating the iconic statues of various political saints that surround the Ontario Parliament, a disconcerting realization settled upon me: this was no longer home.

We moved to the United States sixteen years ago. And while the adage certainly holds true ("You can take the boy out of Canada but you can't take Canada out of the boy"), immigration has repercussions. (If you think moving from Canada to the United States doesn't really count as immigration, well—I'm guessing you're an American.) I am a

"A Peculiar People," *Perspectives: A Journal of Reformed Thought* 26, no. 9 (November 2011): 8–10. Reprinted with permission.

"resident alien" in the country in which I live; but I'm not a resident of the country from which I come. More existentially, that walk around Queen's Park reminded me that while all my memories are Canadian, all my cultural references are American. I can't vote in the elections about which I'm most informed, and I'm not informed about those in which, technically, I could still vote. I'm *between* countries, not quite at home anywhere.

In my denomination, the Christian Reformed Church (CRC) in North America, however, this is hardly a unique experience. Consider the remarkable growth of Korean congregations in our denomination, or Nigerian and Haitian Christians who have made the CRC their home in the United States and Canada, or children from China who have been welcomed into Christian Reformed families. And, of course, there were a few Dutch folk who immigrated to the United States and, later, Canada.

Indeed, the immigrant experience is a very important part of the CRC story. But I worry that we often misunderstand and misconstrue this aspect of the CRC heritage. For example, there are some historians who would almost *reduce* the CRC to the dynamics of immigration. On this account, the CRC emerges as an ethnic denomination, a kind of ecclesiastical ghetto trying to transplant Netherlandish ways into insulated North America enclaves. By reducing ecclesial habits to ethnic memory, such historians tend to explain the distinctives of the CRC as immigrant "hangovers," as quaint habits retained from the old country.

There is a very important upshot of this account: any allegiance to CRC tradition is seen as a covert attempt to cling to the old country. In other words, any defense of distinctive, traditional CRC practice is reduced to immigrant nostalgia. Theological claims are reduced to ulterior motives. In short, if you buy into this story, and run with it long enough, what pretends to be "Reformed" is reduced to being "Dutch."

It seems to me a number of CRC folks have unwittingly bought into this account, which might explain what has always been a curious phenomenon for me: CRC self-loathing. I name this tentatively, as a bit of an elephant in the room. But I suspect many will immediately know what I'm talking about.

This, too, is a common feature of immigrant experience, especially for children of immigrants or "Generation 1.5" (those who immigrated as children). It is the strange embarrassment of being "peculiar": not knowing the language or customs, coming to school with a lunch that smells different, regularly having to translate for your parents, and much more. (Novelist and writer Jhumpa Lahiri is a masterful documenter of the precarious peculiarity of immigrant communities, especially as experienced by children.) Eager to avoid this awkwardness, the children of immigrants are often eager to assimilate and thus distance themselves from the markers of their parents' "old ways."

Because a lot of CRC folk—including, it seems to me, denominational leaders—have unwittingly bought the historians' ethnic reductionism, they have also implicitly accepted the Reformed = Dutch equation. As a result, the dynamics of immigrant embarrassment wash onto our denomination's *theological* heritage. Rightly wanting to unhook the CRC from mere "Dutchness," but having confused Reformed practice with Dutch ethnicity, eager reformers in our denomination advocate throwing overboard all sorts of

Reformed theological distinctives in the name of relevance, reform, and even anti-racism.

Of Babies, Bathwater, and Telling the Difference

We need a different paradigm. We need to refuse the tendency to reduce Reformed identity to mere Dutch heritage. We need to resist accounts that confuse theological distinctives with ethnic habits. I have previously argued in these pages that the CRC needs to do some work sifting our ethnic habits from our theological inheritance. This is a two-edged sword: on the one hand, we can't let merely ethnic preferences masquerade as theological distinctives; that is, we can't allow Dutch traditional*ism* to parade under a Reformed banner.

But I don't think this is our biggest problem today. No, we need to appreciate the second edge of this point: while we cannot allow mere Dutchness to mask itself as Reformed, neither can we jettison the riches of a Reformed theological heritage under the pretense that it is merely an ethnic inheritance. We can't confuse Reformed babies with Dutch bathwater.

What our denomination needs to embrace is *good peculiarity*. Or, to put it otherwise, we should want to be peculiar for the right reasons. Like the children of immigrants, we might sometimes be embarrassed by our peculiarity: our inability to fit in, our sense of not being *quite* at home anywhere, all the ways our family "stands out" as strange. We might be eager to assimilate, to look like others, to mimic the local dialect, to erase our peculiarity.

But peculiarity is prized in Scripture. Indeed, it is almost a synonym for holiness. Consider Peter's description of the people of God in their sojourn among the nations: "You are a chosen people, a royal priesthood, a holy nation, a people belonging to God, that you may declare the praises of him who called you out of darkness into his wonderful light" (1 Peter 2:9). In one of those delightful archaicisms of the King James Bible, "a people belonging to God" is simply translated as "a peculiar people." To be called by God into his covenant people is itself an experience of immigration, emigrating from darkness to light, finding our citizenship in this "peculiar people" that is a "holy nation." We are *called* to be peculiar.

We need to appreciate that many of the habits and practices carried to North America by Dutch forebears were not just ways to cling to an ethnic identity; they were formative practices of holy peculiarity, rooted in Reformed theological convictions and indebted to a Christian heritage much older than the Union of Utrecht. The formative wisdom carried in these Reformed practices is part of our catholic heritage as Christians. They are tangible expressions of holiness with a unique Reformed accent. To abandon them is not a triumphal overcoming of a parochial heritage; it is to spurn the good gifts handed down to us.

Consider just one concrete example. If you talk to some CRC old-timers, you'll inevitably hear some funny stories about what they could and could not do on Sunday. Observing a sabbatarian rule, most CRC communities kept the Sabbath as holy, as a day of rest. This would have all sorts of seemingly arbitrary expressions (which is why CRCers have always enjoyed reading Potok's *The Chosen*). No working, of course—which translated into all sorts of instantiations: no cooking, no cutting the grass, no going to restaurants, no reading "secular" books, no playing baseball, no *watching* baseball, and so on. Admittedly, there seemed to be some hairsplitting: Yes, Henk, you can go in the lake, but only up to your waist, and no jumping up and down! But the practice of Sabbath keeping was not just negative. Rest wasn't just absence of activity, it was also devotion to worship, reflection, catechesis, and fellowship.

Is this just part of an embarrassing ethnic hangover, something they did because they were Dutch? Or did this practice of Sabbath keeping represent a *good peculiarity* that grew out of essentially Reformed expressions of Christian faith? Indeed, one can find some of our most important Christian thinkers today—spiritual writers like Marva Dawn, Dorothy Bass, and Norman Wirzba—reminding the church of the importance of Sabbath keeping as a uniquely Christian practice for resisting the totalitarianism of globalization. Did our forebears perhaps know something we didn't—not because they were Dutch, but because they were Reformed?

The future of the CRC requires that we squarely face the realities of our ethnic heritage(s). But many of the unique strengths and gifts of our Reformed heritage should not be confused with an ethnic inheritance. They are, rather, the gifts of God for the people of God.

4

IS ALL OF LIFE WORSHIP?

Sanctification for Ordinary Life

Whose Protestantism? Which Reformation?

There are many different ways to tell the story of the Protestant Reformation. A favorite angle centers on the heroic tale of Martin Luther, an Augustinian monk newly convicted by his discovery of Paul's forensic gospel, furiously hammering his Ninety-Five Theses to the church door in Wittenberg. The Reformation is thus launched by a kind of medieval blog post about justification by faith that becomes the catalyst for a theological action-adventure narrative filled with public battles, backdoor intrigue, wily villains, and our lone hero declaring, Braveheart-like, "Here I stand!"

There are other sides to the story of the Reformation. A different angle is emphasized by scholars as diverse as

---

"Sanctification for Ordinary Life," *Reformed Worship* 103 (March 2012): 17–19. Reprinted with permission. This essay explores a unique challenge for those indebted to theology of Abraham Kuyper, in particular his notion of "sphere sovereignty"—that society is made up of a number of different "spheres" (the family, the state, the church, commerce, etc.), that each have their own jurisdiction, as it were.

Michael Walzer, Nicholas Wolterstorff, and, most recently, the Canadian philosopher Charles Taylor. This angle on the story sees the Reformation not only as a narrowly theological debate about soteriology but more broadly as a Christian reform movement concerned with the shape of social life—with how we understand our life *coram Deo*, before God.

As Taylor tells the story, the Protestant Reformation was one of several "reform" movements in the late Middle Ages and early modern period that all railed against the distorted social arrangements of medieval Christendom. In particular, the Reformation called into question the "two-tiered" or "multi-speed" religion that had emerged, with "renunciative vocations" on the top tier (monks, nuns, priests), and everybody else mired in domestic ("secular") life consigned to the lower level as second-class spiritual citizens. The "religious" worshiped while everyone else just worked.

In this climate, the really revolutionary impact of the Reformation issued more from Geneva than Wittenberg: calling into question this two-tiered, sacred/secular arrangement, Reformers like John Calvin and his heirs refused such distinctions. All of life is to be lived *coram Deo*, they said—that is, before the face of God. *All* vocations can be holy, for all of our cultural labors can be expressions of tending God's world. There is no "secular" because there is not a square inch of creation that is not the Lord's.

The result is what Taylor calls "the sanctification of ordinary life." On the one hand, this has a leveling effect: the monk is no holier than the farmer, the nun no holier than the mother. Renunciation is no longer seen as the shortcut to divine blessing; if anything, it is seen as perhaps spurning God's good gifts. On the other hand, it's not just that the renunciative vocations are laid low; on the contrary, the expectations are ratcheted up for lay people. Engagement in domestic life is no longer a free pass from pursuing holiness. So while ordinary, domestic life is taken up and sanctified, renunciation is now built into ordinary life. So the butcher, the baker, and the candlestick maker are affirmed in their "worldly" stations as also called to serve God, just like the priest; on the other hand, the domestic laborer does this with something of a mendicant asceticism. It was this interplay of worldly holiness and holy worldliness that Max Weber would later call the Protestant work ethic.

All of Life Is Worship

This "sanctification of ordinary life" is at the heart of the Reformation heritage and is central especially to those streams of the Reformed tradition that emanate from the continent. We are exhorted to do *all* to the glory of God (1 Cor. 10:31). *All* of life can be doxological. All of life can be *worship*. Whether we're in the laboratory or the law office, homemaking or placekicking, tilling the earth or sculpting clay, all of our cultural labors can be expressions of praise to the King. As one of our hymns extols:

> Holy is the setting of each room and yard,
> lecture hall and kitchen, office, shop, and ward.
> Holy is the rhythm of our working hours;
> hallow then our purpose, energy, and powers.
> ("Father, Help Your People," *Psalter Hymnal* 607, v. 2)

However, this principle ("all of life is worship") can be taken to an extreme, especially when conjoined with a sort of mutant Kuyperianism that is a tad vigorous in policing the boundaries between the "spheres"—a Kuyperianism that is more Kuyperian than Kuyper! Then the principle is employed as a premise in an argument that comes to a strange conclusion: since all of life is worship, the argument goes, then the gathered worship of the church seems, well, *optional*, and perhaps even unnecessary. The library and laboratory are on par with the chapel, even preferred over the chapel. On this account, "the sanctification of ordinary life" becomes a directive to vacate the sanctuary.

Is that what the Reformers had in mind? Or do we have here a distortion of the Reformers' impulse, like an extended version of the telephone game in which the Reformers first whisper, "All of life is sacred," only to have the message garbled down the line, finally spoken as "Who needs church?"

Expression *and* Formation

This overreaching of the "all of life is worship" principle is part of a bad habit that we picked up after the Reformation: the tendency to reduce worship to expression. After the Reformation, and especially in the wake of modernity, wide swaths of contemporary Christianity tend to only think of worship as an upward act of the people of God who gather to offer up their sacrifice of praise, expressing their gratitude and devotion to the Father, with the Son, in the power of the Holy Spirit.

Obviously this is an entirely biblical impulse and understanding: if *we* don't praise, even the rocks will cry out. In a sense, we are made to praise. The biblical vision of history culminates in the book of Revelation with a worshiping throng enacting the exhortation of Psalm 150 to "praise the Lord!" However, one can also see how such expressivist understandings of worship feed into (and off of) some of the worst aspects of modernity. Worship as expression is easily hijacked by the swirling eddy of individualism. In that case, even gathered worship is more like a collection of individual, private encounters with God in which worshipers express an interior devotion. It is precisely this model that prizes "authenticity" so highly.

And the same expressivism is behind those versions of the "all of life is worship" principle that see gathered Sunday worship as basically optional—a particularly Reformed version of the spiritual-but-not-religious canard that waxes eloquent about the "church" of nature and the "sacred experience" of a mountain sunrise.

But over the course of Christian history (including the Reformation), worship was always understood as more than expression. Christian worship is also a *formative* practice precisely because worship is also a downward encounter in which God is the primary actor. Worship isn't just something we do; it does something to us. Worship is a space where we are nourished by Word and sacrament—we eat the Word and eat the bread that is the Word of life. This understanding of worship is equally central to the Reformation heritage and is at the heart of John Calvin's legacy.

In fact, one could show that worship is reduced to mere expression just to the extent that we abandon a sacramental understanding of Christian worship. If we fail to appreciate that Word and sacrament are specially "charged" conduits of the Spirit's formative power, it would be easy to imagine worship can happen just anywhere. But if we appreciate that

Christian worship around Word and table is a unique hot spot of the Spirit's wonder-working power, then we also will appreciate that the sanctuary can't be replaced by just any other space in God's good world, for it is in the sanctuary that we are made *into* a people of praise. There is a unique promise of the Spirit that is tethered to Word and sacrament that is received in communal worship.

(In case Kuyperian border patrols are getting worried, it might be helpful to remember that Kuyper himself emphasized this same point. The church as "organism"—engaged in cultural labor—works "in necessary connection with" the church as "institute"—gathered in Christian worship. It is our immersion in the formative practices of gathered Christian worship around Word and sacrament that forms us and equips us to be agents of cultural renewal. The church as organism is no replacement for the church as institute; to the contrary, the organism needs to be nourished by the institute.)

Sanctification *for* Ordinary Life

Christian worship that is gathered around Word and table is not just a platform for our expression; it is the space for the Spirit's (trans)formation of us. The practices of gathered Christian worship have a specific shape precisely because this is how the Spirit recruits us into the story of God reconciling the world to himself in Christ. There is a logic to the shape of intentional, historic Christian worship that performs the gospel over and over again as a way to form and reform our habits. If we fail to immerse ourselves in sacramental, transformative worship, we will not be adequately formed to be ambassadors of Christ's redemption in and for the world. In short, while the Reformers rightly emphasized the sanctification of ordinary life, they never for a moment thought this would be possible without being sanctified by Word and sacrament.

Embedded in this intuition is a helpful, even prophetic, corrective to our triumphalist tendencies. The Reformed vision of cultural renewal can breed its own sort of activism, an almost quasi-Pelagian confidence in *our* work of cultural transformation. In fact, we can sometimes become so consumed with transforming culture and pursuing *shalom* that our well-intentioned activity becomes an end in itself. We spend so much time being the church as organism that we end up abandoning the church as institute. In fact, we not only emphasize that all of life is worship, we come up with self-congratulatory quips that look down on worship as pietistic, as somehow a retreat from the hard, messy work of culture making.

But as Kuyper himself emphasized, there is no way we are going to persist in the monumental task of kingdom-oriented culture-making if we are not being habituated as citizens of the King. As N. T. Wright once counseled in the pages of *Reformed Worship*,

God's work in the world is never merely pragmatic. It isn't simply "We can organize a program to go and do this." If you think we can do God's work like that, read the lives of people like William Wilberforce and think again. You can't. You need prayer, you need the sacraments, you need that patient faithfulness—because we are not wrestling against flesh and blood but against principalities and powers and the world rulers of this present darkness. (*Reformed Worship* 91 [March 2009]: 14)

If we are going to be caught up in God's mission of remaking the world, thereby sanctifying ordinary life, we need to be sanctified by the Spirit through Word and sacrament. If all of life is going to be worship, we need to learn how in the sanctuary.

5

REDEEMING RITUAL

Who's Afraid of Ritual?

Protestants tend to recoil at mention of the *R*-word: *ritual*. The word is a trigger that unconsciously evokes a Reformation history that has sunk into our bones. We associate ritual with dead orthodoxy, vain repetition, the denial of grace, trying to earn salvation, scoring points with God, going through the motions, and various other forms of spiritual insincerity.

And yet we affirm, even celebrate, ritual in other spheres of our lives. We recognize that the pursuit of excellence often requires devotion to a regime of routines and disciplines that are formative precisely because they are repetitive. Anyone who has mastered a golf swing or a Bach fugue is a ritual animal: one simply doesn't achieve such excellence otherwise. In both cases, ritual is marked by *embodied repetition*. Ritual recruits our will through our body: the cellist's fingers become habituated by moving back and forth through scale after scale; the golfer's whole body is trained by a million practice swings.

"Redeeming Ritual," *The Banner* 147, no. 2 (February 2012): 18–19.

Because we are embodied creatures of habit—and were *created* that way by God—we are profoundly shaped by ritual. That's why ritual can *de*-form us, too: we witness, or know firsthand, the destructive power of routines and rhythms that can hold us captive and make us someone we don't want to be.

In all of these cases we implicitly intuit that rituals are not just something that we do; they do something *to* us. And their formative power works on the *body*, not just the mind. So why should we be so allergic to ritual when it comes to thinking about our spiritual life? Could we redeem ritual? Let me try.

Habitations of the Spirit

Our negative evaluation of ritual stems from a couple of bad assumptions. First, when it comes to religious devotion, we tend to see ritual observance as mere obedience to duty, a way of scoring points with God and earning spiritual credit. We see ritual as a bottom-up effort—and it's just that notion of "effort" that starts to sound like "work," and it doesn't take long before this all seems part of an elaborate system of salvation by works.

Let's grant that some religious folk undoubtedly observe ritual with such misguided intent. We join Luther and Calvin and the Reformers in rejecting such superstitious attempts to curry God's favor. But why should we settle for simply *identifying* ritual with works righteousness? Why should Pelagians get to own ritual?

We have a more nuanced take on ritual in other spheres of our life. We can tell when someone is "just going through the motions," but we don't thereby see the motions themselves as the problem. For example, we can tell the difference between the piano student practicing scales because she has to and the student who does so in pursuit of excellence. While some might enter ritual as a merely bottom-up duty, others appreciate *why* the ritual is important: not just because it is an expression of my devotion but because it is a means by which I am shaped and formed and transformed.

If I commit myself to the ritual of playing scales for an hour a day for years on end, it's because I know this is a way for me to become something I *want* to be. It's because I see the ritual not just as something I do but as a formative practice that does something *to* me. The ritual is not just a bottom-up exercise on my part; it's also a kind of top-down force that makes me and molds me. I'll see the ritual as a way for me to be caught up in the music—a way for my fingers and hands and mind and imagination to be recruited into the symphony that I want to play.

If that is true on a natural level, why shouldn't it also be true when it comes to our spiritual life? Historic Christian devotion bequeaths to us rituals and rhythms and routines that are what Craig Dykstra calls "habitations of the Spirit"—concrete practices that are conduits of the power of the Spirit and the transformative grace of God.

Think of some ho-hum rituals in Reformed worship. In some congregations, week after week we are asked to stand to hear the Word of God. Why? That shift in our bodily posture sends a little unconscious signal: something important is coming—listen up. And after we hear the Word, the preacher announces: "This is the Word of the Lord." To which we reply, "Thanks be to God." You might take that for granted. You might even say it without thinking about it. But that doesn't mean it's not *doing* something: it is a tiny little ritual that trains your body to learn something about the authority of God's Word, and to respond in gratitude.

Spirit-charged rituals are tangible ways that God gets hold of us, reorients us, and empowers us to be his image bearers. They are ways for the Spirit to meet us where we are—as embodied creatures, not disembodied angels.

Worship Is for Bodies

A second reason we devalue ritual is because we reduce Christianity to a set of beliefs. We tend to treat Christian faith as a primarily heady affair and see believers as primarily "thinking things." In fact, Reformed folk often have the corner on this market.

The Canadian philosopher Charles Taylor describes this "intellectualism" as one of those Frankensteinish outcomes of the Protestant Reformation—a sort of unintended monster that outruns any of the good intentions of the Reformers themselves. Rightly criticizing superstition and magical views of ritual, the Reformers unleashed an impetus toward what Taylor calls "excarnation"—a *dis*-embodiment of spiritual life that reduced true religion to right belief.

The result was eventually a complete reconfiguration of worship and devotion. Gradually, Christian worship was no longer a full-orbed exercise that recruited the body and touched all of the senses; instead, Protestants designed worship as if believers were little more than brains on a stick. The primary target was the mind; the primary means was a long, lecture-like sermon; and the primary goal was to deposit the right doctrines, beliefs, and ideas into our heads so that we could then be sent out into the world to carry out the mission of God.

The problem, however, is that we were not created as brains on a stick. We are not merely thinking things. We are created as embodied, tactile, visceral creatures who are more than cognitive processors or belief machines. Such excarnation is a denial of our (good) embodiment. As full-bodied image bearers of God, our center of gravity is located as much in our bodies as in our minds. This is precisely why the body is the way to our heart, and it is this "incarnational" intuition that has long informed the rich history of spiritual disciplines and liturgical formation.

Some of this we already do. Those congregations that celebrate the Lord's Supper weekly (as John Calvin prescribed for Geneva) have a deep appreciation for the tactile nature of the practice. Here is a ritual that pictures the gospel, that activates every one of our senses: taste, touch, smell, hearing, and sight. It is a ritual whose repetition is a gift, not a bore. And because of its holistic nature, the gospel sinks into our bones through our immersion in the ritual. We absorb the story of God's grace in ways we don't even realize.

Or consider a simple ritual that might be especially appropriate for Lent: rituals of confession. I would encourage congregations to see the value of adopting a form of confession that involves both repetition and the body. By adopting a standard prayer of confession, worship constantly puts a prayer on our lips that seeps into our hearts. As such, it will also be a prayer that comes forth from our heart through the week. And when a congregation *kneels* to confess, our physical posture both expresses and encourages our humility before our God. We will know God's grace differently because it will be inscribed in our bodies.

We need not be afraid of ritual. If we appreciate that God created us as incarnate, embodied creatures, then we will see that his grace is lovingly extended to us in ways that meet us where we are: in the tangible, embodied practice of Spirit-charged rituals. Reframed in this way, we might be able to redeem rituals as gifts of God for the people of God.

6

THE CASE FOR CHRISTIAN EDUCATION

It's commonly noted that as members of the Christian Reformed Church fanned out across North America, they first built churches, then built schools. In communities from Ancaster, Ontario, to Bellflower, California—or from Edmonton, Alberta, to Patterson, New Jersey—school bells arose alongside steeples. Sanctuaries were constructed alongside classrooms. And families who gathered for worship on Sunday saw each other all week long at the local Christian school.

Is this just a quaint historical oddity—the patterns of an immigrant community trying to carve out little colonies in the intimidating new world? Or is there a more integral connection between Reformed faith and Christian education? And if so, then wouldn't Christian education be as important today as it was in the 1880s or the 1950s?

These are important questions to ask. Each generation

"The Case for Christian Education," *The Banner* 145, no. 8 (August 2010): 20–21. Reprinted with permission.

needs to re-own the rationale for Christian education, which requires that we ask ourselves: Why *did* we do this? And should we *keep* doing this? If the answers of a past generation don't stand up today, then perhaps we need to rethink the project of Christian schooling.

So why Christian schools? Why were earlier generations committed to Christian education, investing in schools in often sacrificial ways? The rationale was biblical, comprehensive, and radical. Stemming from the biblical conviction that "the fear of the LORD is the beginning of wisdom" (Ps. 111:10 NRSV), the Reformed tradition (and the CRC in particular) has long recognized that Christ's lordship extends over every sphere of life, including education. There is no sphere of life that is neutral; rather, our practices and institutions are always and ultimately shaped and informed by faith commitments. So while an institution might claim to be "secular," as if it were *not* religious, Reformed thinkers from Abraham Kuyper to Nicholas Wolterstorff have seen through such claims: what pretends to be neutral or secular in fact masks some other faith commitment.

It's in this sense that the vision of Christian education is *radical*: it stems from the conviction that any and every education finds its *root* (Latin *radix*) in some worldview, some constellation of ultimate beliefs. Therefore, it's important that the education and formation of Christians be rooted in Christ (Col. 2:7)—rooted in and nourished by a Christian worldview across the curriculum. The commitment to Christian schooling grows out of a sense that to confess "Jesus is Lord" has a radical impact on how we see every aspect of God's good creation. The curriculum at Christian schools enables children to learn about everything—from algebra to zygotes—through the lens of Christian faith.

Now, it might be helpful to point out what Christian education is *not*. First, Christian education is not meant to be a merely "safe" education. The impetus for Christian schooling is not a protectionist concern, driven by fear, to sequester children from the big, bad world. Christian schools are not meant to be moral bubbles or holy huddles where children are encouraged to stick their heads in the sand. Rather, Christian schools are called to be like Aslan in the *Chronicles of Narnia*: not safe, but *good*. Instead of antiseptic moral bubbles, Christian schools are moral incubators that help students not only to see the glories of creation but also to discern and understand the brokenness of this fallen world. While the Christian classroom makes room for appreciating the wonders of God's good world in the stunning complexity of cell biology and the rich diversity of world cultures, it also is a place to understand the systemic injustices behind racism and the macroeconomics of poverty. Christian schools are not places for preserving a naïve innocence; they are laboratories to form children who see that our broken world is full of widows, orphans, and strangers we are called to love and welcome. In short, Christian schools are not a withdrawal from the world; they are a lens and microscope to see the world for what it is in all its broken beauty.

Second, Christian schools are not just about Bible classes. The curriculum of a Christian school is not simply the curriculum of a public school *plus* religion courses. While Christian education provides a wonderful opportunity to deepen knowledge of God's Word, it's not Bible class that makes the school Christian. Rather, the Reformed vision of Christian education emphasizes that the entire curriculum is shaped and nourished by faith in Christ, "for by him all things were created: things in heaven and on earth, visible and invisible, whether thrones or powers or rulers or authorities; all things were created by him and for him. He is before all things, and in him all things hold together" (Col. 1:16–17). Christian schools are not just extensions of Sunday School focused on learning religion; they are Christ-rooted educational institutions focused on religious learning.

Third, Christian education is not a merely "private" education. Christian schools are not meant to be elite enclaves for the wealthy. To the extent that Christian schools have become merely pious renditions of prep schools, they have failed to appreciate the radical, biblical calling of Christian education. Those forebears who built schools alongside churches were committed to Christian education *for all*. In *Our World Belongs to God: A Contemporary Testimony*, we confess that

> In education we seek to acknowledge the Lord
> by promoting schools and teaching
> in which the light of his Word shines in all learning,
> where students, of whatever ability,
> are treated as persons who bear God's image
> and have a place in his plan.

This brings us back to a crucial feature of this vision of Christian education. While the decision about schooling rests with families, the project of Christian education involves an entire community. Christian schooling takes a village—to nourish the vision, to form Christian teachers, and to help share the burdens of costs and risks. Thus CRC communities have understood a commitment to Christian schools as an expression of the promises we make at baptism—an expression of our covenant to be the "village" that supports the formation and education of our children. And this finds very tangible expression in a unique practice of kingdom economics where, like the early church (Acts 4:32–36), the entire community shares the economic burden of Christian schooling. They do so by pooling resources in a concrete picture of solidarity, where older generations support younger generations through giving to the Christian education fund, grateful for the generations before them that did the same. Only such a gift-giving economy can make it possible for Christian education to be a blessing for all members.

Let's be honest: Christian schooling is a high-investment, labor-intensive venture. It requires sacrifices and hard choices. And it is increasingly countercultural to pursue such a vision. But when it is carried out in the best spirit of the Reformed tradition—when Christian education is an intentional, intensive, formative curriculum bent on shaping young people as agents and ambassadors of God's coming kingdom—the investment proves to be wise stewardship.

So it turns out that Christian education is not just a 19th-century hangover. It is a project that bubbles up from the very nature of the church as a covenant community, and it is an expression of core convictions of the Reformed tradition. And we might need it now more than ever.

7

LEARNING (BY) STORIES

A Future for Christian Education

It is an honor to be able to join you as you celebrate 100 years of Christian schooling here at Northern Michigan Christian School. I never cease to be amazed by the communities that sustain Christian schools, against so many odds and off the radar of our cultural mainstream. According to so many metrics, you shouldn't still be here! Economic pressures, community fatigue, and the trajectory of secularization all make the reality of Christian schools a veritable institutional miracle.

But whether it's McBain, Michigan, or Waupun, Wisconson, or Smithville, Ontario, these Christian school communities are a testimony to a God who is faithful to his peculiar people. And they are testimony to a Spirit-led

"Learning (by) Stories: A Future for Christian Education," *Christian Educators Journal* 51 (2011): 4–9. Reprinted with permission. This was originally an address given at Northern Michigan Christian School in McBain, MI, as part of its 100th anniversary celebration. I'm grateful to Dirk Walhout for the opportunity to see the good work happening at NMCS.

people who are committed to goods beyond their bottom line—who so value the formation of their children that they are willing to set aside other pleasures of "the good life" in order to provide a faith-full education for their young people. The centenary of Northern Michigan Christian School is a witness that you are a community invested in "tell[ing] the next generation the praiseworthy deeds of the LORD" (Ps. 78:4).

This would be an easy time to get nostalgic—to wistfully recall the old days, some golden age gone by, to pine for the way things were—which usually comes with a kind of resignation that those days are gone, that we're just waiting for the inevitable dwindling and denouement. But Christians have a very different sense of *time*: in the words of that immortal Michael J. Fox movie, God calls us "back to the future." When God constantly enjoins his people to *remember*, he is always asking them to remember *forward*, to remember for the sake of the future. Yahweh presses Israel to remember the covenant and their liberation from Egypt, not so they can wallow in wistful memories of bobby socks and letterman jackets and kvetch about the "good ol' days." They are called to remember because God is calling them *to* something—to the promised land.

We need to appreciate how countercultural this sense of time is. We live in an age that is easily attracted to nostalgia. Whether it's our fascination with *Mad Men* or our fixation on the Founding Fathers, we are easily duped into hiding in an idealized past. Indeed, just recently I read of a strange new phenomenon: the adult prom. This would be funny if it weren't about the saddest thing I've ever heard of: adults with children and mortgages and minivans trying to relive their adolescence, largely because they inhabit a culture that has encouraged them to never grow up.

When Christians remember, we are not retreating to the past; we are being catapulted toward a future. God's people inhabit time in this strange tension, where we are called to remember so that we can *hope*. When Jesus enjoins us to eat and drink in remembrance of that Last Supper, he also points us toward the future: we celebrate the Lord's Supper "until he comes," and so the remembrance is really just a foretaste of that coming feast. Our traditions are the gifts that propel us toward the future with hopeful expectation. Christians inhabit time as a *stretched* people.

So let's not confuse a celebration of faithfulness with a mere trip down memory lane. Let's use this as an occasion to think about the future of Christian education, to hope with God-sized expectations about what the Spirit is going to continue to do here at Northern Michigan Christian School—because Christian education isn't just something that's nice while it lasts; it might just be crucial for future of the people of God. Indeed, I think Christian schooling is an incredible opportunity in our postmodern context, and it might be more important now than ever.

I would like to make this case by considering the centrality of *story* to Christian education. Christian education tells the story of God's redemption; indeed, Christian education is another way of inviting young people *into* that story. But we also need to appreciate that we learn *by* stories.

Learning by Stories

Let me begin with what might sound like a disconcerting

thesis: Christian education is not fundamentally about *knowledge*. Christian schooling is not primarily about the dissemination of information. Education is not only or fundamentally about filling our intellects. And this is because we are not primarily thinking things. Students are not brains on a stick, with idea-receptacles just waiting to be filled with information.

No, we are not thinking things; we are *lovers*. God has made us by and for love. As Saint Augustine prayed in his opening to the *Confessions*, "You have made us for yourself, and our hearts are restless until they rest in you." In this biblical picture of the human person, the core of our being is the *heart*, the seat of our passions, desires, and longings— the fulcrum of our love. And it is out of the heart that our action flows. While we tend to assume that we *think* our way through the world, in fact it is our love that governs and drives our action. The center of gravity of the human person isn't located in the head, it's located in the gut. So the most formative education is a pedagogy of desire.

While we are what we love, *what* we love is precisely what's at issue. Our love can be aimed at very different ends. We can desire very different kingdoms. While we are made to love God and his kingdom, we are prone to wander, looking for love in all the wrong places. So our love needs to be *trained*; our desire needs to be schooled. This is why, in his letter to the Philippians, the Apostle Paul first prays for their love: "And this I pray: that your love may abound still more and more in real knowledge and all discernment, so that you might determine *what really matters*" (Phil. 1:9–10, my translation). Love precedes knowledge. Not only do I believe in order to understand, I love in order to understand.

So our most basic and fundamental and formative education is a *sentimental* education—an education of our sentiments, our love and desire. The *New York Times*, columnist David Brooks has described this as our "second" education. In a recent column, he put it this way:

> Like many of you, I went to elementary school, high school and college. I took such and such classes, earned such and such grades, and amassed such and such degrees.
>
> But on the night of Feb. 2, 1975, I turned on WMMR in Philadelphia and became mesmerized by a concert the radio station was broadcasting. The concert was by a group I'd never heard of—Bruce Springsteen and the E Street Band. Thus began a part of my second education.
>
> We don't usually think of this second education. For reasons having to do with the peculiarities of our civilization, we pay a great deal of attention to our scholastic educations, which are formal and supervised, and we devote much less public thought to our emotional educations, which are unsupervised and haphazard. This is odd, since our emotional educations are much more important to our long-term happiness and the quality of our lives.[1]

There are two things to take away from Brooks's account: first, what he's calling our "second" education—our "sentimental" education—is actually the most fundamental, the most basic. It makes the biggest difference. Second, if Brooks was schooled by Bruce Springsteen, then this sort of affective education happens *everywhere*. This sort of sentimental education is not confined to classrooms and lecture halls. This education spills over our institutional barriers—our sentiments are being educated all the time. Our culture is rife with pedagogies of desire.

Now what does this have to do with Christian education? Well, at least two things: First, we need to realize that the competitor for Christian education is not the public schools—it is all of the pedagogies of desire that are operative across our culture, in all of the secular liturgies we're immersed in that covertly form our loves. If a Christian education is going to contribute to the formation of kingdom citizens, then it needs to be a *counter*-formation, countering the pedagogies of desire that would aim our love at rival versions of the kingdom. We—and our children—are immersed in affective sentimental educations all over the place: at the concert, in the cinema, at the stadium, at Walmart, or on the National Mall. These are loaded spaces that come charged with their own vision of the good life, their own implicit vision of the kingdom. These are not just places to go and things to do; they do something *to* us: they educate our hearts, often apprenticing us to a disordered, rival vision of the good life. And over time, that education works on us—those rival visions of flourishing seep into us ever so slyly, very much under the radar of our intellects. If an education is going to be Christian, it has to be a *re*-training of our hearts, a counterformation to these secular liturgies.

But this brings us to a second implication: at their best, Christian schools are precisely the sorts of educational institutions that *get* this. In other words, in the very DNA of Christian schooling is already an intuition about the importance of our second, sentimental education. Listen again to Brooks:

> This second education doesn't work the way the scholastic education works. In a normal school-room, information walks through the front door and announces itself by light of day. It's direct. The teacher describes the material to be covered, and then everybody works through it.
>
> The knowledge transmitted in an emotional education, on the other hand, comes indirectly, seeping through the cracks of the windowpanes, from under the floorboards and through the vents. . . . The learning is indirect and unconscious. . . .
>
> I find I can't really describe what this landscape feels like, especially in newspaper prose. But I do believe [Springsteen's] narrative tone, the mental map, has worked its way into my head, influencing the way I organize the buzzing confusion of reality, shaping the unconscious categories through which I perceive events. Just as being from New York or rural Georgia gives you a perspective from which to see the world, so spending time in Springsteen's universe inculcates its own preconscious viewpoint.

Brooks can't quite imagine a school that isn't just "scholastic"; he can't quite imagine a school that provides a "second" education. But that, it seems to me, is precisely the mission and vision of Christian schools. Christian education is a holistic vision for the formation of the whole person, equipping minds *and* forming hearts, educating our love by aiming our desire toward God and his kingdom. What should distinguish Christian education is just this *holism* precisely because a biblical picture of the person helps us appreciate both theory and practice, both cognition and affect, both knowledge and desire. An integral Christian education doesn't separate head and heart, intellect and emotion. Christian schools are unique precisely insofar as they very intentionally offer both a first *and* second education. And such schools are nested in other communities of practice like the church and home, which are partners in this other education.

So what does this have to do with *stories*? Well, our hearts traffic in stories. Not only are we lovers, we are also storytellers (and storylisteners). As the novelist David Foster Wallace once put it, "We need narrative like we need space-time; it's a built-in thing." We are narrative animals whose very orientation to the world is most fundamentally shaped by stories. Indeed, it tends to be stories that capture our imagination—stories that seep into our heart and aim our love. We're less convinced by arguments than moved by stories. The philosopher Alasdair MacIntyre says that stories are so fundamental to our identity that we don't know what to do without one. As he puts it, I can't answer the question "What ought I to do?" unless I have already answered a *prior* question, "Of which story am I a part?" It is a story that provides the moral map of our universe.

Stories, then, are not just nice little entertainments to jazz up the material; stories are not just some supplementary way of making content interesting. No, we learn through stories because we know *by* stories. Indeed, we know things in stories that we couldn't know any other way: there is an irreducibility of narrative knowledge that eludes translation and paraphrase.

In his discussion of education among the people of Israel in *The Creative Word*, Old Testament scholar Walter Brueggemann captures the point: in the Torah, when a child asks a question, the teacher's response is "Let me tell you a story." For the people of God, he continues, story "is our primal and most characteristic mode of knowledge. It is the foundation from which come all other knowledge claims we have."[2]

So the task of Christian schooling is nested in a story—in the narrative arc of the biblical drama of God's faithfulness to creation and to his people. It is crucial that the *story* of God in Christ redeeming the world be the very air we breathe, the scaffolding around us, whether we're at our Bunsen burners or on the baseball field, whether we're learning geometry or just learning to count. All of the work of the Christian school needs to be nested in this bigger story—and we need to constantly look for ways to tell that story, and to teach *in* stories, because story is the first language of love. If hearts are going to be aimed toward God's kingdom, they'll be won over by good storytellers.

Learning Stories

A holistic Christian education invites students into the incredible story of what God is doing in Christ, redeeming and restoring and renewing this broken but blessed world. As a whole education, Christian schooling embeds students in a community whose practices—ideally—function as compressed, embodied performances of this story. Such

Christian schooling stages the drama of redemption and invites students—indeed, all of us—to see ourselves in the play. Christian schools are one of the "actors studios" that train the people of God to play a part in this "act" of the drama of redemption. To receive a Christian education is to learn this story, not just as a bit of information stored in our heads, but as an entire imagination that seeps into our bones.

But I would add one final role for story in Christian education. If we are going to invite future generations into this adventure that is Christian schooling, we need to share stories about it. If Christian education is going to have a future, it needs to be *attractive*—and the attractional pull will not come from airtight arguments or legalistic rules or data about outcomes. If Christian education is going to continue to capture the imagination of future generations, they will be captured by the *stories* we tell. Indeed, the alumni of our schools will be the living epistles that embody this story. Telling their stories will provide a winsome witness to the unique *formation* they received in Christian schools.

Let me close with one of my own stories, not because it's earth-shattering or exemplary, but because I just want to try to put some flesh on these bones. I could tell you all kinds of stories about academic excellence and rigorous learning. I could also share wonderful experiences of a curriculum rooted in a big vision of God's care for his creation, equipping students to be ambassadors of his kingdom in every sphere of culture. I'd be happy to testify to the concern for justice that my children have absorbed through their Christian education. Let's take that for granted. Instead, I want to give you a peek at what's unique but almost intangible about Christian education.

The story comes from an episode almost ten years ago. When we moved to Grand Rapids from Los Angeles, one of our children had a particularly difficult transition. We had sort of underestimated the angst our relocation had generated for him, and we didn't quite understand that all his acting out was his way of trying to grapple with this disorientation. The notes and calls coming home were a steady stream of concern. We worried that he'd wear out his welcome at Oakdale Christian School before he ever really got started!

It came time to attend our first parent-teacher conference with Mrs. Braman. We were braced for the experience, expecting to be both scolded and embarrassed. We were ready to face the music about our failure as parents. So we sat down with Mrs. Braman and she quickly announced, "I *love* your son." We tried to point out to her that we were the Smiths—was she perhaps expecting a different family? Had we shown up at the wrong appointment? But what we quickly learned was this: she *loved* our son. She loved our son because she was a teacher caught up in the messy narrative of redemption, the story of God's gracious love in Christ, the drama of God's hope for this broken world. She loved our son because she knew that our gracious God plays a long game and isn't surprised by anything. And she saw in our son the disciple in the making, the follower of Jesus buried in all his fear and bewilderment. And she loved him.

And for my son, that wasn't just care; it was an education. He saw love modeled. He intangibly absorbed aspects of God's story through his teacher's example of the virtues. He received a second education in that experience, which has trained his own love and compassion. This was one part of an embodied curriculum that taught him, over the years, what really matters—that God's kingdom is concerned with the marginalized, the outsiders, the vulnerable, even though Mrs. Braman didn't *say* a word about that. That sort of education happens every day, and over a lifetime, in schools like Northern Michigan Christian School. And we can't afford to lose it.

So as we celebrate 100 years of God's faithfulness to Northern Michigan Christian School, let's not just saunter down memory lane. Let's remember in order to hope—to hope and expect even bigger things from the Spirit who loves to surprise us. Let's be that community that sees Christian schools as an arm of the very *mission* of God. With outsized hope let's imagine how *all* God's children could be shaped and formed by such an education. Let's renew the sacrificial love of generations past who made it possible for us to be celebrating here today. As a community of faith, caught up in the story of God in Christ, let's recommit ourselves to our baptismal promises, with a renewed passion for Christian schooling not as a private education but as a sentimental education, an education of the heart and a pedagogy of desire. Let's embrace Christian education as the counterformation that is crucial for the future of the church's mission in the world. And let's not just *tell* the next generation; let's *show* them.

Notes

1. David Brooks, "The Other Education," *New York Times*, November 26, 2009: www.nytimes.com/2009/11/27/opinion/27brooks.html.

2. Walter Brueggemann, *The Creative Word: Canon as a Model for Biblical Educaton* (Philadelphia: Fortress, 1982), 22–23.

Part

2

LINES OF ARGUMENT
Books and Culture

D ESPITE ALL OF THE APOCALYPTIC NEWS WE HEAR
about the end of the book and the demise of reading, the fact remains that books are still an important en-
gine of cultural change and commerce. So engaging—and
reviewing—books is a critical way to engage culture, especially when this can be done not in venues that are sequestered behind the paywalls of specialized peer-reviewed
journals but rather in periodicals that reach wider audiences. In such venues, one is usually trying to simultaneously speak to other scholars *and* write for practitioners and
laypeople who have an investment in the matters at hand. So
most of the chapters in this section are about ideas, but they
were most immediately occasioned by books that deserved
attention, response, and in some cases, critique.

   This is also why the essays in this section tend to be
the most polemical. Sometimes they draw lines in the sand.
In other cases they'll claim that someone has crossed the
line. In every instance, you'll find a clear line of argument

(it's usually no secret what I think). But as I noted in the introduction, I don't think polemics and charity are dichotomous: rather, sometimes it is precisely love for the body of Christ that calls for the staunchest polemics. I'll leave it to the reader to discern whether I've crossed the line in that respect.

8

How (Not) to Change
the World

Whose Transformation? Which Assimilation?

It's hard to resist the spectacle of the Wachowski brothers'
film *Speed Racer*. Their visual evocation of a kind of live-
action anime hovers and wavers between surrealism and
camp. For those of us raised on *G-Force*, the allure of this
aesthetic is palpable yet unexplainable.

But in addition to this aesthetic allure, I am also
tempted to read the film allegorically, strangely intrigued
by a melodramatic, almost cliché line uttered by Racer X
to the eponymous Speed: "It doesn't matter if racing never
changes. What matters is if racing changes us."

The context is the corporate corruption of the World

"How (Not) To Change the World," a review of James Davison Hunter,
*To Change the World: The Irony, Tragedy, and Possibility of Christianity in
the Late Modern World* (New York: Oxford University Press, 2010), first
published in *The Other Journal* (September 8, 2010). Reprinted with permission.

Racing League, which is rife and systemic. The WRL has always been this way, and Speed despairs that winning *within* the system will not change the system—indeed, that perhaps nothing can change the system. But at the same time, both X and Speed have a compulsion to race, and that compulsion can only work itself out within the system. (One might say that the corrupt system owns all the tracks.) So given that context and compulsion, the question becomes an issue of assimilation: "What matters is if racing changes us." While this might sound like a kind of Stoicism, I don't think it is: Speed and his entire family, devoted to racing, are trying to imagine racing otherwise and are trying to embody a different kind of team, a different kind of racing, and a different kind of practice within the corporate system. But if X is right, one doesn't necessarily work out this impulse in order to transform the system. Maybe "it doesn't matter if racing never changes." Perhaps what's at issue is whether racing changes us. And perhaps this could be read as a parable about Christianity and American culture.

Many of us are more indebted to James Davison Hunter than we might realize. His 1991 book, *Culture Wars*, has been a lens through which many have understood the dynamics of American politics, even if they have never read it. An astute and influential observer of American culture, particularly the role of (and transformation of) religion in the public sphere, Hunter is a sociologist without the usual allergy to normative language. And while he's never taken sides in the culture wars (indeed, despite the way it is cited by both friends and detractors, *Culture Wars* was pointing out the futility of conducting such battles), Hunter has not shied away from prescription rooted in description and analysis. Thus, his later book *The Death of Character* unapologetically laments the loss of a unified moral ethos in American culture that undercuts the possibility of true character formation. Although Hunter's writing can sometimes tend toward the curmudgeonly end of the jeremiad spectrum, he's nonetheless an important cultural critic.

His latest offering is a logical trajectory from this earlier work. *To Change the World* is explicitly addressed to Christians in the United States and is his most unabashedly prescriptive and theological work to date. It is also one of the most important works on Christianity and culture since Nicholas Wolterstorff's *Until Justice and Peace Embrace*. One could hope that *To Change the World* might finally displace the lazy hegemony of Niebuhr's *Christ and Culture*, even if I think Hunter's book might have a couple of similar faults.

It is, above all, a timely book: Hunter is out to do nothing less than displace the dominant Christian understanding of culture and cultural change, with the hope of radically revising Christian strategies for cultural engagement. The targets here are varied but specific: both the Christian Right and Left are subject to criticism because of their very penchant for "changing the world." But anticultural fundamentalists and acultural evangelicals who neglect culture making altogether are also objects of critique. Hunter is an equal opportunity offender, which should give us a clue that he's onto something different. This is not a tired rehearsal of old party lines. But let me first provide a map of the book before diving into more substantive issues.

Rethinking Cultural Change

To Change the World is organized into three multichapter essays. By describing them as "essays," Hunter gives himself permission to paint with broad brushstrokes, to write with a strong voice, and excuses himself from any responsibility to exhaustively peruse the literature. But that does not absolve him of responsibility altogether; he's still very much offering an argument. And while pedantic scholars may complain about a thousand missing details, Hunter's strategy here is just right. These are big questions, and he needs the elbow room of the essay in order to make his case.

The first essay is a critique of the dominant understanding of culture and cultural change, particularly as assumed by Christians who see themselves engaged in the mission of "changing the world." And I suppose one has to appreciate just how extensively such lingo has come to permeate evangelical institutions, particularly parachurch organizations with political interests, but also Christian colleges and universities.[1] Hunter's critique of talk about "transforming culture" and "changing the world" can be withering, as seen in his opening critique of Chuck Colson's influential manifesto *How Now Shall We Live?* But Hunter is no respecter of misguided strategies and is equally critical of Catholic or leftish versions of the same project. When it comes to mistaken conceptions of cultural change, Jim Wallis has nothing on Chuck Colson, Hunter argues.

The problem is that such projects for transforming culture assume a naïve and idealistic view of culture and cultural change. Their view is idealistic because it places too much priority on *ideas*; they mistakenly assume that culture is made up of an accumulation of heady things like ideas and beliefs and values—that culture is akin to a "worldview" (pp. 6, 24–26).[2] Working with this idealist assumption, people like Colson and Nancy Pearcey adopt a "hearts and minds" strategy because they mistakenly assume that the "culture war" is a "*cognitive* war" (p. 25). And they assume that if we can change the hearts and minds of individuals, we'll change the culture (or "reclaim" the culture, as the rhetoric often goes).

For Hunter, such a strategy is benighted because it assumes a simplistic notion of culture and cultural change. Culture, he argues, is not the sort of thing that resides in sets of propositions (p. 33); rather, culture is more like an infrastructure than an intellectual framework—more like an environment than a set of ideas. Even more importantly, Hunter emphasizes that culture—and hence cultural change—is most profoundly shaped and determined by centers of power. "In other words," he bluntly summarizes, "the work of world-making and world-changing are, by and large, the work of elites" (p. 41). This makes grassroots efforts at cultural change among "the people" (like, say, Sarah Palin's "real Americans") misguided and doomed to failure—which is just to say that most of the mass efforts of Christian parachurch organizations can expect the same. Indeed, for Hunter this explains just why all these Christian efforts (and dollars) have failed to halt the slide toward secularization and fragmentation in American society.

It's not that ideas don't have consequences, only that there are conditions under which ideas *might* have consequences: "Ideas do have consequences in history, yet not because those ideas are inherently truthful or obviously correct but rather because of the way they are embedded in very powerful institutions, networks, interests, and symbols" (p. 44).[3] Hunter tries to make this case with a long historical survey (ch. 5) and then compares this with the paltry cultural output of American Christianity over the past century (ch. 6). As a populist movement, and (rightly) allergic to elitism, evangelicalism has either eschewed cultural production altogether or has instead engaged in merely *sub*cultural production—generating the mimicking kitsch that fills Christian "gift" stores across the country. Such subcultural production (that is, the production of an evangelical subculture) actually betrays that "large swaths [of evangelicalism] have been captured by the spirit of the age" (p. 92). No matter how many Jesus action figures or Hipster Study Bibles™ we might sell, the battle's already been lost as soon as such phenomena exist. All we've done is carve out a new market sector that extends dominant cultural forces. This is a long way from "changing the world," despite our rhetoric to the contrary. The world has changed us.

What starts to emerge, then, is a twofold problem: on the one hand, those who want to "change the world" are working with naïve conceptions of culture and cultural change; on the other hand, such world changers tend to be allergic to power and suspicious of elitism. Hunter's second essay, then, is a kind of "power therapy," meant to disabuse Christians of naïve understandings of cultural change and also to help them work through their "power issues," as it were. It is in this essay that Hunter articulates his critique of both the Christian Right and Christian Left (what there is of it!), noting the "civil religion of the left" (pp. 145–48).[4] It is this critique of civil religion that motivates his serious engagement with "neo-Anabaptists" like Stanley Hauerwas who, Hunter argues, are exactly right in diagnosing the error of Right/Left ways but are still misguided because they valorize "powerlessness" (p. 181). Because, according to Hunter, if the church really wants to *change* the world, and not fall into merely assimilated subcultural renditions of it, then Christians need to get over their allergy to power and elitism. "The question for the church," Hunter emphasizes, "is not about choosing between power and powerlessness but rather, to the extent that it has space to do so, *how will the church and its people use the power that they have.* How will it engage the world around it and of which it is a part?" (p. 184; emphasis original). Decoupling the public from the political,[5] and looking at Jesus as an exemplar of the exercise of power, Hunter sets up the constructive proposal sketched in the third essay.

It is in the third essay that Hunter gives us a Niebuhr-like taxonomy, summarizing three paradigms of Christian engagement with culture as "defensive against," "relevance to," and "purity from" (pp. 213ff.). It is generally conservative Christians who are "defensive against" culture, "constructing a complex empire of parallel institutions" (p. 214) while still covertly hoping to repristinate America as a Christian nation. "Relevance to" culture has historically been the strategy of accommodating liberalism, but Hunter rightly points out that the same accommodation to culture happens in seeker-sensitive evangelicalism. Finally, those who want to preserve "purity from" culture are a motley crew: on the one hand, Hunter includes pietistic evangelicals and Pentecostals from the holiness tradition; on the other hand, it's also here that he locates the neo-Anabaptists described earlier—one of his most problematic claims. Indeed, this whole categorization is one of the less nuanced strategies in the book; and although he simply offers this overview as a heuristic device, one can worry that—like Niebuhr's taxonomy—the cost of simplicity isn't worth it.

But apart from problems with these categories, I'm primarily interested in Hunter's constructive proposal for a different paradigm: "faithful presence within." This paradigm is first sketched much earlier in the book, at the conclusion of the first essay. In that context, we can appreciate Hunter's concerns and in what sense "faithful presence" is an alternative to the other paradigms. On the one hand, his model of faithful presence is deeply concerned about the extent of Christianity's assimilation to American culture, even in the name of being "conservative."[6] What's wrong with both the Christian Right and Left, Hunter rightly notes, is that they have unwittingly bought into the will to power that characterizes disordered political life in late modern America. As a shorthand, one can say (as Hunter sometimes does) that they have fallen prey to a Constantinian desire to run the world (or at least America). The problem is that, in the name of "reclaiming America for Christ," their "Christ" has been assimilated to what we might call "Americanism"—or what Hunter will sometimes describe simply as "nihilism" (p. 264).[7] Faithful presence, then, is not simply a kind of baptism of Nietzsche's will-to-power in Jesus's name, bent on seeing Christianity triumph in the culture war. Indeed, faithful presence will often run counter to the strategies of religious politics as currently played. Instead, faithful presence is the church carrying out the creational mandate to make culture (Gen. 1:26–31) in a way that is faithful to God's desires for his creation. As such, "the best understanding of the creation mandate is not about changing the world at all. It is certainly not about 'saving Western civilization,' 'saving America,' 'winning the culture war,' or anything else like it" (p. 95). Rather, "the church is to bear witness to and to be the embodiment of the coming Kingdom of God"—to be a foretaste of the new creation. And that "new" creation "is a reference to the kingdom of God working in us and in the world; a different people and an alternative culture that is, nevertheless, integrated within the present culture" that includes "networks (and more, communities) of counter-leaders operating within the upper echelons of cultural production and social life generally" (p. 96).

This emphasis on antithesis and the critique of Constantinianism make Hunter deeply sympathetic to the neo-Anabaptists (pp. 150–66). In fact, this is one of the most refreshing, even courageous aspects of his book. However, Hunter's model of faithful presence also cuts against what he takes to be the weakness of the neo-Anabaptist paradigm. When he's speaking against the Religious Right/Left, Hunter emphasizes that Christians are called to *faithful* presence rather than Constantinian dominance. But when he turns to the neo-Anabaptists, Hunter emphasizes that Christians are called to faithful *presence* rather than sectarian absence or withdrawal. Whereas the Constantinianism of the Christian Right/Left neglects the radical antithesis of faithfully following Jesus's model of cruciform power, Hunter thinks that the neo-Anabaptists neglect the cultural mandate. Although the neo-Anabaptists rightly emphasize antithesis, he thinks they lack a fundamental "affirmation" of "culture and culture-making having their own validity before God that is not nullified by the fall" (p. 231). Because of this, "they ignore the implications of the incarnation in the vocations of ordinary Christians in the workaday world" (p. 223).[8] Whether this is a fair characterization of the neo-Anabaptist paradigm will be a matter of discussion below; here it is important to appreciate that Hunter takes his model of faithful *presence* to be an alternative to models that neglect the God-given task of culture making more broadly.

In this respect, Hunter's model of faithful presence resonates with a long tradition of Reformed reflection on culture that has emphasized the creational goodness of culture making.[9] "A theology of faithful presence," he concludes, "obligates us to do what we are able, under the sovereignty of God, to shape the patterns of life and work and relationship—that is, the institutions in which our lives are constituted—toward a shalom that seeks the welfare not only of those of the household of God but of all" (p. 254). This will inevitably require stewardly exercise of power and not merely a supposedly "Christian" version of the will to power bent on winning.[10] Rather, "the *means of influence* and the *ends of influence* must conform to the exercise of power modeled by Christ" (p. 254; emphasis original).

So how do we change the world? Wrong question, Hunter argues (p. 285). The desire to change the world too easily tends toward reactive strategies of *ressentiment* and ends up playing by the rules of the will to power. So instead we should be asking, What does faithful culture making look like? What does it mean for us to care for the gardens—and cities—in which God has placed us? When that is our concern, change will be a by-product at best. Hunter summarizes this in an important, italicized passage:

*If there are benevolent consequences of our engagement with the world, in other words, it is precisely because it is **not** rooted in a desire to change the world for the better but rather because it is an expression of a desire to honor the creator of all goodness, beauty, and truth, a manifestation of our loving obedience to God, and a fulfillment of God's comment to love our neighbor.* (p. 234)

Continuing the Conversation

I am deeply sympathetic to both Hunter's diagnosis and constructive proposal. If it's too much to hope that this book could displace Niebuhr's *Christ and Culture* from college syllabi, I at least hope *To Change the World* will be treated as a must-read companion volume. More importantly, I hope Hunter's argument might tame the rhetoric of "transforming culture" which has so captivated evangelicalism over the past decade, given that so often such language is really only a cover for further assimilation. In sum, *To Change the World* could be a game changer for conversations about Christianity and culture.

That said, in the spirit of continued reflection on these important matters, let me highlight a couple of themes as a springboard for further conversation in a more critical mode. Encouraging more nuance in his analysis and argument, I offer some criticisms in the spirit of an assist.

First, I worry that Hunter's critique of the neo-Anabaptists remains a critique of a caricature. I say this cautiously because I applaud his critical appreciation for the neo-Anabaptist critique of Constantinian strategies (Hunter includes Radical Orthodoxy under the Constantinian banner, which is debatable but defensible). As already noted, Hunter worries that the neo-Anabaptists give up on culture making altogether, thus ending up with a separatist or sectarian concern for purity. But do neo-Anabaptists such as John Howard Yoder and Stanley Hauerwas really lack a theological affirmation of culture making?[11] I don't think so.[12] Indeed, I think the neo-Anabaptist paradigm (particularly in its "Radically Orthodox" version[13]) is *very* close to Hunter's own model of faithful presence.

The confusion (and thus perceived distance) between Hunter and the neo-Anabaptists might stem from equivocation about the term *world*. Even within the canon of Scripture, this is a slippery term.[14] And I worry that Hunter misreads the neo-Anabaptists by *over*-reading their critique of "the world" *as if* it were a critique of creation per se.[15] For example, when Hunter claims that neo-Anabaptists make "a sharp dichotomy between the church and the world" (p. 160),[16] he seems to read this as if they posited a sharp dichotomy between the church and creation (and, hence, culture), thereby also positing a problematic tension between the orders of redemption and creation.[17] Conversely, when Hunter claims that "there is a world that God created that is shared in common by believers and nonbelievers alike" (p. 232), the "world" he's naming there is not "the world" being rejected by the neo-Anabaptists. On the one hand, "world" names the disordered cultural systems of a fallen world "under the control of the evil one" (1 John 5:19); on the other hand, "world" can be used to name the space of the created cosmos, the "territory" of creation. If we fail to discern and distinguish these different meanings, we'll end up reading the neo-Anabaptist critique of "the world" as if it were a kind of Gnosticism—which Hunter unfortunately does (p. 251). Whereas, in fact, Hunter's proposal for the church creating "an alternative culture . . . within the present culture" (p. 96) could be a very fitting summary for much of the neo-Anabaptist vision of faithful culture making.[18] All this is just to say that Hunter might find allies where he least expects them.[19] And I suspect that if neo-Anabaptists carefully and charitably considered Hunter's articulation of a Jesus-centric theology of power, they *might* be willing to consider how and why impacting elite culture might be faithful—though that's going to be a hard habit to break.

Related to the proximity of Hunter's position and a noncaricatured neo-Anabaptist model is a second point of concern: if our calling is to faithfully make culture in a way that embodies God's desires for his creation and is a foretaste of the coming kingdom, and if, as a result, we're not primarily concerned with changing the world but with making culture in a way that is faithful, then it's not clear to me why so-called "parallel institutions" can't be instantiations of faithful presence. And yet Hunter is persistently critical of parallel institutions.

Now many so-called "Christian" parallel institutions are worthy of critique because, rather than being sites of faithful culture-making, they are merely syncretistic examples of subcultural mimicry—"Jesufied" versions of the majority culture. Let's agree that such substandard, subcultural institutions are worthy of critique. But other parallel institutions might be generated because they are the only way and place to carry out faithful culture making without being severely compromised by the disordered systems of a majority culture. Insofar as such parallel institutions are still in the world (i.e., solidly located in the territory of creation), they can clearly still bear witness to what creation is called to be, thus fulfilling the obligation of faithful presence. To criticize parallel institutions *tout court* feels like a transformationist hangover, a still-quasi-Constantinian worry that we're neglecting our responsibility to be custodians of the (majority) culture. But if that were the case, then it sounds like Hunter still wants to win—still wants to change the world—whereas perhaps what matters is that we "race well," so to speak, and not let the world change us.

Notes

1. We also should try to appreciate how *recent* this consensus is. See my discussion of Greg Boyd's *Myth of a Christian Nation* in *The Devil Reads Derrida: And Other Essays on the University, the Church, Politics, and the Arts* (Grand Rapids, MI: Eerdmans, 2009), 97–101.

2. Anyone familiar with my argument in *Desiring the Kingdom: Worship, Worldview, and Cultural Formation* (Grand Rapids, MI: Baker Academic, 2009) will sense a healthy degree of overlap in our concerns here. What's intriguing, from my standpoint, is that Hunter and I end up in the same place, with the same critique of "worldviewism," but seem to have arrived there from quite different trajectories.

3. One can thus see how Redeemer Presbyterian, pastored by Tim Keller in New York City, is seeking to be a witness amid one of the centers of cultural power in the United States. However, one also needs to appreciate Hunter's nuance on this point, as he is very critical of the story that Michael Lindsay tells about *Faith in the Halls of Power*: "The idea that significant numbers of Christians are operating 'in the halls of power' in ways that are thoughtful and strategic . . . is simply ludicrous" (p. 274; cf.

p. 306n25). So it's not just about getting into the halls of power; it's also about *what* you do (and why you're doing it) once you get there.

4. In a similar vein, I have criticized what I describe as a "Constantinianism of the Left" in *The Devil Reads Derrida*, 105–12.

5. "Politics is just one way to engage the world and, arguably, not the highest, best, most effective, nor most humane to do so" (p. 185).

6. Hunter rightly diagnoses this as a matter of *formation*: "The problem for Christians—to restate the broader issue once more—is not that their faith is weak or inadequate. . . . But while they have faith, *they have also been formed by the larger post-Christian culture*, a culture whose habits of life less and less resemble anything like the vision of human flourishing provided by the life of Christ and witness of scripture" (p. 227; emphasis original). Thus, if the church is going to carry out its mission of "faithful presence," it will have to consider its practice of formation and counterformation. This is precisely my concern in *Desiring the Kingdom*, where I suggest that evangelicalism has become assimilated to American culture precisely because evangelicals have failed to appreciate the formative power of "secular liturgies." See Smith, *Desiring the Kingdom*, 89–129.

7. I especially appreciate Hunter's willingness to name our complicity with a "market society" where "the logic, language, and ideals of rational and free exchange based on a calculation of costs and benefits spill out of the economy proper and into the entire culture thus shaping every sphere of social life. . . . In the case of the mega-churches or the seeker church movement in Evangelicalism, the embrace of a market rationale is the deliberate foundation of its strategy" (p. 264). The problem is that "this kind of autonomous instrumentality is also fundamentally nihilistic" (ibid.).

8. A related concern is the neo-Anabaptist valorization of "powerlessness," which Hunter interprets as an abdication of creational responsibility (p. 181).

9. Indeed, one of the oddities of the book is the complete absence

of Abraham Kuyper from the discussion. I note this, not as a failure to be comprehensive (I respect the "essay" genre), but only because where Hunter ends up is so close to Kuyper's model (even if Hunter is rightly critical of Chuck Colson's bastardization of Kuyper in *How Now Shall We Live?*). That said, I also think Hunter's emphasis on antithesis is a refreshing break from the tendency of late modern Kuyperians to overemphasize affirmation under the rubric of common grace.

10. Hunter's criticism is pointed: "The tragic irony is that in the name of resisting the dark nihilisms of the modern age, Christians—in their will to power and the *ressentiment* that fuels it—perpetuate that nihilism. In so doing, Christians undermine the message of the very gospel they cherish and desire to advance" (p. 275).

11. I grant that Hunter has cited passages from Robert Brimlow (p. 250) that do seem guilty of just this. I'm just not sure Brimlow is representative in this respect.

12. For a comprehensive account of Yoder's affirmative theology of creation and culture, see Branson Parler, *Things Hold Together: John Howard Yoder's Trinitarian Theology of Culture* (Harrisonburg, VA: Herald Press, 2012).

13. See especially the work of Graham Ward, in his most recent book, *Political Discipleship: Becoming Postmaterial Citizens*, Church and Postmodern Culture Series (Grand Rapids, MI: Baker Academic, 2009).

14. For discussion of this point, see Smith, *Desiring the Kingdom*, 187–90.

15. In a similar way, Hunter seems to make the common mistake of equating Augustine's "earthly city" with creational life per se (p. 161). Thus, Hunter takes a critique of the earthly city to be a critique creaturely life. But that's clearly not the case for Augustine given that the origin of the "earthly city" is not creation but the fall. I hope to demonstrate this more fully elsewhere.

16. Later in the book he calls this their "hermetic distinction between church and world" (p. 182).

17. The latter is a common Reformed critique of Yoder, which Parler has now shown to be patently false.

18. In a similar way, Hunter fails to appreciate the neo-Anabaptist claims about "the politics of Jesus" (per Yoder) and the church as *polis*. He reads this as yet another reduction of Christianity to politics "as with the Christian Right and Left" (p. 163), whereas Yoder and William Cavanaugh are imagining politics otherwise—again, in a way very similar to Hunter, it seems to me. Like Hunter, they are equally concerned to reject the statecraft that has tempted the Christian Right and Left.

19. In this context, let me also note that I would (now) agree with Hunter that while there should be a recognition of radical antithesis, this does not preclude the possibility of finding ad hoc occasions for strategic collaboration (in reference to his discussion of a point from my *Introducing Radical Orthodoxy* on pp. 332–33 of *To Change the World*). Following Augustine (and Oliver O'Donovan), I would agree that we can find points of penultimate overlapping concern. I hope to expand on this point in a forthcoming work on Augustine.

9

THINKING BIBLICALLY
ABOUT CULTURE

There is a subtle irony in the fact that a book by a liberal theologian has so thoroughly suffused contemporary evangelical self-understanding. H. Richard Niebuhr's *Christ and Culture* has achieved the status of a classic not because it has been particularly influential among his mainline confreres, but because his taxonomy of various Christian understandings of "culture" has become a template for evangelical introspection. Wittingly or unwittingly, the spate of recent books that articulate the evangelical mission of "transforming culture" are working with the lexicon of a neo-orthodox theologian.

Its status as a veritable evangelical classic has also generated critique, including Craig Carter's incisive *Rethinking Christ and Culture* (Brazos, 2007), and here D. A. Carson's *Christ and Culture Revisited*. Carson rightly seeks to revisit

---

This first appeared as "Christ and Culture and Creation and Church," a review of D. A. Carson, *Christ and Culture Revisited* (Grand Rapids, MI: Eerdmans, 2008), at *Christianity Today* online (October 2008). Reprinted with permission.

Niebuhr's categories; more specifically, refusing to take them as a given, Carson holds their feet to the biblical fire. As a biblical theologian, he is concerned that Niebuhr's categories have taken on a life of their own, achieving such independent status that Christians now take up his models without considering how (or whether) they grow out of biblical wisdom. Carson also suggests that Niebuhr's strategy is a bit like recent discussions of the atonement: for too long, various models of the atonement were considered to be mutually exclusive, whereas the richness of the biblical vision might best be honored by embracing them as complementary understandings of Christ's work on the cross. So, too, with models of Christ and culture, Carson suggests. Perhaps we should stop feeling compelled to pick and choose among them and instead consider a bigger picture that integrates these different approaches together (pp. 61–62, 206).

Carson is also rightly concerned to detach accounts of "Christ and culture" from the American provincialism that often attends such analyses. As he wryly puts it, "If Abraham Kuyper had grown up under the conditions of the killing fields of Cambodia, one suspects his view of the relationship between Christianity and culture would have been significantly modified" (pp. ix–x). Thus Carson brings up other contexts where Christians must wrestle with these questions, such as France and other European environs, but also sectors of the majority world where Christians face persecution and political environments that are a long way from Western democracy. As such, he hints at a more global consideration of the question.

His core project, however, is to root a Christian understanding of culture and cultural engagement in the narrative of Scripture. Carson's persistent point is that Christian thinking about culture must be explicitly and positively informed by "the great turning points in salvation history" (p. 67). In a way, this approach highlights the fact that *Jesus* makes remarkably few appearances in Christian understandings of culture; instead, we get significant appeals to creation, justice, and so forth. As Carson notes, "However loyal one judges oneself to be to Jesus, it is difficult to see how such loyalty is a mark of *Christian* thought if the Jesus so invoked is so domesticated and selectively constructed that he bears little relation to the Bible" (p. 44). Carson invites us to ask: are we really dealing with a *Christian* account of culture if the *cross* never shows up? In the name of "Christian" approaches to culture, we get a lot of *creational* models, but very few *cruciform* approaches. On this score, I think Carson and Carter might agree.

Unfortunately, it is precisely in its Scriptural aspirations that the book falters. For one, Carson's "overview" of the biblical narrative is remarkably piecemeal and selective, and it ignores some significant biblical passages that seem crucial for such an analysis, such as 1 Peter 2:9, Acts 2:44–46 and 4:32–37, and Old Testament passages such as Jeremiah 7 and 21. In addition, his tendency to make one pronouncement of Jesus ("Give back to Caesar what is Caesar's") a veritable canon within the canon undercuts the very canonical emphasis that motivates his project. But it is Carson's theology that lies at the root of the problem.

Given the riches of biblical wisdom across its canonical sweep, Carson's plot summary of the story is puzzling. While he emphasizes the doctrine of creation—that "God made everything" (p. 45)—he nowhere attends to what has commonly been described as the cultural mandate, the call embedded in creation for humans to cultivate the earth (Gen. 1:27–29): to unfurl and unfold the possibilities latent within creation through cultural work. Instead, Carson tends to treat "culture" as some sort of given, failing to offer a theology *of* culture that sees the work of human making as rooted in creation itself. I don't think one can just chalk this up to lacking space to deal with all the details. Rather, it indicates a particular take on the "turning points" of redemptive history. A weak theology of creation will lack a clear theology of culture as a task given to humanity *as* image bearers of God. This perhaps explains why, for Carson, "culture" always seems to be a noun (something *out there*) rather than a verb (something we *do*).

It also becomes clear in Carson's survey of redemptive history that *what* is being redeemed are persons: this is "salvation history" (p. 67) and it is "we"—that is, we humans—who are being saved. Because sin is understood narrowly as personal moral transgression and idolatry (pp. 46–48), redemption is conceived in equally narrow terms as the salvation of human persons (pp. 50, 64, 215n24, 217). Because institutions, systems, and structures are absent from Carson's account of creation, they also tend not to show up on the radar of fallenness and redemption. It is "we" who are fallen and "we" who are saved.

It thus comes as no surprise to see an old familiar bifurcation between redemption and "cultural" labor in Carson's understanding of the church's mission—or, as he puts it, "what *the church as church* is mandated to do" (p. 172; emphasis original). And what is that? Well, it's churchy stuff: "When the church meets together in the New Testament," he observes, it is to praise and sing, to teach and learn, to observe the ordinances of baptism and the Lord's Supper, and to exercise discipline—all with a view to equipping the saints for evangelism (pp. 150–51). (I seem to notice the early church also engaging in the redistribution of resources and self-consciously constituting itself as a distinct political community, but never mind.) Carson is clear that the central Christian obligation is ministry and evangelism: when Christians make ministries of compassion and justice central, "they marginalize their responsibilities as members of *the church* of Jesus Christ, the church that lives and dies by the great commission." While Christians might engage in a little cultural engagement on the side, they are called "first and foremost" to be "gospel Christians, deeply engaged in their local churches, extraordinarily disciplined in their own Bible reading and evangelism" (pp. 152–53).

Carson concludes that "the only human organization that continues into eternity is the church" (p. 217). This confirms the narrow eschatology hinted at earlier in the book when he claims that "what must be feared and avoided at all costs is the second death (Revelation 20–22). This means that the current relations between Christ and culture have no final status. These must instead be evaluated in the light of eternity" (pp. 58–59). One senses that Carson's "eternity" lacks cultural institutions—an eternity without commerce or politics, art or athletics. (While he occasionally tips his hat to other areas, Carson's analysis pretty much reduces culture to politics.) All that will remain is "the church," although it is not clear just what the church will be doing since, according to Carson, "the church lives and dies by the great commission" (p. 152). Such a flattened vision of our redeemed future is the correlate of a stunted understanding of creation.

In sum, Carson's laudable project of pushing conversations about "Christ and culture" to the riches of the biblical narrative is a missed opportunity—a missed opportunity to articulate a biblical theology of culture as a creational task, and so also a missed opportunity to finally undo the old bifurcation between the cultural mandate and the great commission. Even those who affirm both too often see them as distinct and fail to discern their intimate connection. For what is the gospel but God's call and invitation to be restored and renewed as image bearers of God? Being God's image bearers is not a static property of being human but a calling, a vocation, and a task, as Richard Middleton has brilliantly laid out in *The Liberating Image* (Brazos, 2005). Christ, as the second Adam, is the Son who has imaged for us what it means to be God's vice-regents: he has shown us what it looks like to *do* this. Christ's death and resurrection have made it possible for us to once again take up our creational calling to be culture makers, re-equipped for the task given to humanity at the start. And Christ has also shown us that, in a fallen and broken world, the shape of that vocation is cruciform: being cultural agents of the crucified God is not a project of triumphal transformation but of suffering witness. The church will be the church when it sees its commitment to the great commission as a matter of extending God's invitation to redemption and renewal, which is precisely an invitation to once again become what we were made to be: God's subcreators.

10

POSER CHRISTIANITY

When I was a teenager, I was religiously devoted to freestyle BMX: flatland, street, vert, all of it. It was my first real experience of something like a spiritual discipline. Every spare moment was spent on my bike; even in long Canadian winters, I carved out a space in our basement to keep riding. I custom-built a bike from select components, studied all the magazines, constructed my own quarter-pipe in the backyard, even published a 'zine for the emerging community of riders in my town. In my senior yearbook, my photo was accompanied by a cheesy maxim lifted from a Harley-Davidson ad: "I live to ride. For those who understand, no explanation is necessary. For those who don't, no explanation is possible."

For the small tribe of religiously devoted BMX freestylers, for whom riding was a way of life, there was nothing more grating or irritating than an even larger tribe that grew up around us: the tribe of posers—that band of kids who

---

"Poser Christianity" was first published as a review of Brett McCracken, *Hipster Christianity: When Church and Cool Collide* (Grand Rapids: Baker Books, 2010) in *The Other Journal* (Winter/Spring 2011): 146–51.

were taken more with the accessories than with the experience. The posers were the group of rich kids who had all the best equipment, wore the latest shoes, sported the latest styles, and then generally spent their time sitting on the sidelines while the rest of us actually *rode* our bikes. They would scramble their bikes to the top of the ramp, but never actually drop in for a round. They'd be using all the right lingo on the deck of the pool, but never inch over the coping. They'd mull around the parking lot talking a big game, but never actually ride. They didn't really want to ride; they were just after a look, an identity by association.

I invoke this scene because I think *poser* is a relevant, important term missing from Brett McCracken's lexicon in *Hipster Christianity: When Church and Cool Collide.* And in very important ways, McCracken's project is lexical. He spends several preparatory chapters amassing a catalog of terms that will be regularly used in the book: cool, hip, trendy, fashionable, relevant, savvy, stylish, even "supercool." But because this lexicon doesn't include *poser*, McCracken's analysis ends up being reductionistic: he thinks anyone who looks like a "hipster" is really just trying to be "cool." This, I think, tells us more about Mr. McCracken than it does about so-called hipster Christianity.

The general upshot of McCracken's book seems to be remarkably similar to Tullian Tchividjian's *Unfashionable*—namely, that Christians should be wary of trying to be *au courant* lest the desire to be "with it" trump the peculiarity and strangeness of the gospel.[1] In short, being cool is dangerous because, in the process, the peculiar people of God become assimilated to the status quo. In this respect, the conclusion to *Hipster Christianity* reads like a gentler rendition of the more strident rants we've heard from people like D. A. Carson and David Wells (the latter of whom is generously cited in the last three chapters of the book). The only difference is the target: whereas Wells and Carson (rightly, I should add) criticized the therapeutic, seeker-sensitive Willow Creeks and Saddlebacks of the boomer generation, McCracken sets his sights on his own generation: hip millennials who are taken with incense, hemp clothing, Wendell Berry, and Amnesty International. McCracken is worried that this is just the next generation of cultural assimilation in the name of relevance.

But his analysis only works if, in fact, all hipsters are really just posers. That is, McCracken effectively reduces all hipsters *to* posers precisely because he can only imagine someone adopting such a lifestyle *in order to be cool.* Let me say it again: this tells us more about McCracken than it does about those young Christians who are spurning conservative, bourgeois values.

I would think McCracken is too young to be this cynical. So I suggest something else is at work here: what we have in *Hipster Christianity* is a jaded ethnography written by someone who spent a youth-group lifetime trying to be one of the cool kids. As such, it seems he can only imagine someone adopting a hipster lifestyle in order to strike a pose. This is confirmed by a crucial turn in the book: McCracken identifies the "birth of the Christian hipster" in 2003, "when the first issue of *Relevant* magazine was released" (p. 88). Well, this explains quite a lot. Did I mention that McCracken was also a longtime contributor to *Relevant* magazine? If *Relevant* magazine is the epitome and embodiment of Christian hipsterdom, then pretty much everything

McCracken says makes sense. *Relevant* magazine is simply the latest in a long line of evangelical subcultural production: derivative, secondary, reactionary, and dependent on wider cultural trends, all with the hopes of showing that following Jesus doesn't really require one to be a loser. Indeed, the magazine's very title is a signal that this is just the continuation of the seeker-sensitive project of the megachurch. Its edgy rendition of evangelical faith doesn't really displace the fundamental, core values of a constituency still comfortable with the status quo of bourgeois American individualism, consumerism, nationalism, and militarism. In other words, being a *Relevant* hipster is the sort of thing you can *add* to your life without really disrupting the rest of it. It's a style, not a way of life.

But let me be very clear now: *Relevant*-magazine hipsters are really just posers. Like all the posers hanging around the half-pipes of my youth, these are people looking for cool by association, with a slight thrill of rebellion as a side-effect. And while McCracken's analysis perhaps pertains to a bunch of suburban kids who have adopted hipster as a style—just as they might have adopted "urban" as a style—his analysis doesn't even touch those students I know who, *from Christian convictions*, have intentionally pursued a lifestyle that rejects the bourgeois consumerism of mass, commercialized culture. They shop at Goodwill and Salvation Army because they have concerns about the injustice of the mass-market clothing industry, because they believe recycling is good stewardship of God's creation, and frankly, because they're relatively poor. They're relatively poor because they're pursuing work that is meaningful and just and creative and won't eat them alive, and such work, although not lucrative, gives them time to spend on the things that really matter: community, friendship, service, and creative collaboration. And despite McCracken's misguided claims about autonomy and independence (pp. 192–93), the Christian hipsters I know are actually willing to sacrifice the American sacred cow of privacy and independence, living in intentional communities as families and singles, working through all the difficulties and blessings of "life together" as Bonhoeffer describes it. In short, the lives of the Christian hipsters I know are a gazillion miles away from being worried about image or trendiness; they live the way they do because they are pursuing the good life characterized by well-ordered culture making that is just and conducive to flourishing—and this requires resisting the mass-produced, mass-marketed, and mass-consumed banalities of the corporate ladder, the suburban veneer of so-called success, as well as the irresponsibility of perpetual adolescence that characterizes so many twentysomethings who imagine life as one big frat house.

This is why I think McCracken needs to revitalize another term in his lexicon: *bohemian* (he mentions it early on, confusing it with *dandyism*). Although he generically talks about Christian hipsters, there is a qualitative difference between a Shane Claiborne and the latest rendition of the megachurch youth pastor who slums it by buying a few things at Goodwill (to accessorize his jeans from the Buckle) and who presses his kids to donate to the ONE Campaign. Those who really deserve to be described as Christian hipsters might be better described as Christian bohemians who have intentionally resisted the siren call of the status quo, upward mobility, and the American way in order to pursue lives that are just, meaningful, communal, and peaceable. The Christian hipsters I know are pursuing a way of life that they (rightly) believe better jives with the picture of flourishing sketched in the biblical visions of the coming kingdom. They have simply discovered a *bigger* gospel: they have come to appreciate that the good news is an announcement with implications not only for individual souls but also for the very shape of social institutions and creational flourishing. They have come to appreciate the fact that God is renewing *all* things and is calling us to ways of life that are conducive to social, economic, and cultural flourishing as pictured in the eschatological glimpses we see in Scripture. They resonate with all of this, not because it's cool, but because it's true.

To be blunt (because I'm not sure how else to put this), the Christian bohemians I'm describing are *educated* evangelicals. So when McCracken lists (not so tongue-in-cheek) "ten signs that a Christian college senior has officially become a Democrat" (p. 159), I'm sorry but the list just looks like characteristics of an educated, thoughtful Christian (and believe me, I'm no Democrat). Or when McCracken, in a remarkably cynical flourish in the vein of "Stuff White People Like," catalogs the authors that Christian hipsters like (Stanley Hauerwas, Ron Sider, Jim Wallis, Flannery O'Connor, Walker Percy, Wendell Berry, N. T. Wright, G. K. Chesterton, and others; p. 97), he does so as if people could only "like" such authors because it's "cool" to do so. But perhaps they're just *good*. McCracken seems unable to really accept what *Paste* magazine editor Josh Jackson emphasizes: "It's not about what's cool. It's about what good" (p. 92). And if that's true, then it should be no surprise that Christian colleges and universities are shapers of Christian hipster culture: if McCracken is lamenting the fact that Christian colleges are producing alumni who are smart and discerning with good taste and deep passions about justice, then we're happy to live with his ire. The fact that young evangelicals, when immersed in a thoughtful liberal arts education, turn out to value what really matters and look critically on the way of life that has been extolled to them in both mass media and mass Christian media—well, we'll wear that as a badge of honor.

In contrast to the Christian bohemian commitment to a good life that reflects the shape of kingdom flourishing, McCracken's concluding chapters read like a naïve, slightly whiny appeal to protect Jesus-in-your-heart evangelical pieties—which, of course, can sit perfectly well with the systemic injustice that characterize "normal" American life. While McCracken is focused on what he takes to be the hipster fixation on appearance (do we really need any more confirmation that McCracken doesn't get it?), he calls us to remember "what *really* counts: our inner person" (p. 203; emphasis original). This is the beginning of pages and pages of tired evangelical clichés ("People should look at us and want what we have" [p. 209]) that culminate in his individualist account of "being a Christian," which means "being transformed," et cetera. So "how can we go on living like we did before once we have become Christians? And how can we possibly live like everyone else in the world when something so radical and transformative has happened in our lives?" (p. 212). Yes, Mr. McCracken, that is indeed the question. And that's exactly why my Christian bohemian friends refuse to live like all of those American evangelicals who have just appended a domesticated Jesus to the status quo of the so-called American Dream. Whereas it turns out you're just worried that young Christians might be (gasp!) smoking and drinking a bit too much and have not sufficiently considered injunctions about dress in 1 Peter 3. Well, yes, indeed: those do seem like quite pressing matters for Christian witness in our postsecular world. By all means, let's get our personal pieties in line. For as McCracken sums it up, "the Christian hipster lifestyle has become far too accommodating and accepting of sin" (p. 200)—and by this, he means a pretty standard litany of evangelical taboos (did I mention sex?). It's funny: my Christian hipster friends think conservative evangelicals have also become too accommodating and accepting of sin, but they tend to have a different inventory in mind—things like the Christian endorsement of torture and wars of aggression, evangelical energies devoted to policies of fiscal selfishness, and lifestyles of persistent, banal greed.

I think the reason these concerns don't show up in *Hipster Christianity* is because McCracken lacks a theology of culture, and because of that, he has a tin ear for the issues of systemic (in)justice that really define the bohemian lifestyle of what we might call authentic hipsters. Indeed, while he tries to berate Christian hipsters for being individualists, McCracken's understanding of Christianity is almost hopelessly individualist, fixated on matters of personal piety and individual salvation. Within that frame, authentic Christian hipsters don't make much sense; such a life could only be a style, a pose. But precisely because McCracken lacks a sufficient theology of culture, and hence lacks any attention to systematic (in)justice, most of the Christian hipsters I know will never read this book. But all of the posers will.

Notes

1. See Tullian Tchividjian, *Unfashionable: Making a Difference in the World by Being Different* (Colorado Springs, CO: Multnomah Books, 2009).

Part 3

BRUSHSTROKES AND LINE BREAKS

On Art, Poetry, and Literature

I N THE CONCLUSION TO HIS IMPORTANT BOOK, *BAD RE-ligion: How We Became a Nation of Heretics*, the *New York Times* columnist Ross Douthat cites a claim made by Joseph Ratzinger shortly before becoming Pope Benedict XVI: "The only really effective apologia for Christianity comes down to two arguments, namely, the saints the Church has produced and the art which has grown in her womb."[1] As anyone who has read my *Desiring the Kingdom* or *Imagining the Kingdom* might guess, I deeply share this conviction. If the gospel is going to be heard by a new generation, it can't just convince intellects; it must capture imaginations.

This is why I think Christian cultural analysis has to include a serious engagement with the arts—not just as instrumental ways to package religious claims, but as genuine expressions of what creational flourishing might look like. Furthermore, I believe the church needs to move beyond its obsession with the *au courant* of pop culture and reinvest in those cultural forms that ask more of us: poetry, the novel, painting, and more. The chapters in this section take up contemporary work in poetry, literature, and aesthetics, taking seriously the intersection of brush strokes and line breaks with the very power of transcendence.

Notes

1. Ross Douthat, *Bad Religion: How We Became a Nation of Heretics* (New York: Free Press, 2012), 292.

11

SHOW ME THE WORLD

Of late there has been a stream of Christian cultural criticism that encourages conservative evangelicals to "look for God" in contemporary culture. Exhorting us to overcome a rather Manichean dissection of the world into holy and profane, this mode of cultural engagement encourages us to "find God" in contemporary music, Hollywood movies, and various forms of popular culture.

I'm not convinced this is the best hermeneutic frame for appreciating the arts. It still tends to instrumentalize the arts as a conduit for a gospel message or theistic propositions. The result is too often a fixation on God language in cultural artifacts or—worse—belabored allegorical readings that see "Christ figures" everywhere.

We should expect art to be more oblique. And instead of asking artists to show us God, we should want them to reveal the world—to *expand* the world, to *make* worlds that expand creation with their gifts of co- and subcreative power.

"Show Me the World," an engagement with Charles Wright's *Sestets* (New York: Farrar, Straus and Giroux, 2009), first appeared at *Comment* online (July 30, 2010). Reprinted with permission.

The calling of painters and poets, sculptors and songwriters, is not always and only to hymn the Creator but also and often to be at play in the fields of the Lord, mired and mucking about in the gifted immanence that is creation. With that rich creational mandate, a Christian affirmation of the arts refuses the instrumentalist justification that we "find God" in our plays and poetry. In a way that is provocatively close to the aestheticism of Walter Pater and Oscar Wilde, such a creational framing of the arts grants license for art to be quite "useless"—to (almost) be art for its own sake, for the sake of delight and play, for the sheer wonder and mystery of creating. Some of our best artists show us corners of creation we wouldn't have seen otherwise—and often because they've just given birth to a possibility hitherto only latent in the womb of creation.

Unhooking the arts from a theological instrumentalism also grants space for the arts to reveal the brokenness of creation without being supervised by a banal moralism. A painting or a poem *reveals* the world with a harrowing attention that will sometimes bring us face-to-face with what we've managed to willfully ignore up to that point.

In sum, the arts can be a means of what we might call "horizontal" revelation without necessarily being connected to "vertical" revelation. Like the book of Esther, God might never show up. Nonetheless, the Creator might best be honored when we face up to the puzzling, mysterious nuances of his creation.

This is why I have become a devotee of the poetry of Charles Wright—not because I "find God" in his poetry (though he does make some cameos, often in the second person, like in prayers), but because through his poetry I see the world again, the world that's been in front of me this whole time. Wright's worlds are multiple: Tennessee and northern Italy on dark nights and bright shiny mornings, in conversation with Rorty, Virgil, and Walter Benjamin. He loosens things up in a strangely playful sobriety. Indeed, Wright's most recent collection, *Sestets*, is downright proverbial. Over the course of the book, the compact, repeated form of six lines (the second division of an Italian sonnet, *per* Petrarch) takes on an aphoristic lilt tinged with silver-crowned wisdom.

There's a conceit running through *Sestets* that tackles the revelatory vocation of the poet. Wright considers this under the rubric of "description," that attentive unpacking of creation that is at the heart of so many of these poems. The ruse begins with impossibility, as in the poem "Outscape," which opens: "There's no way to describe how the light splays / after the storm, under the clouds"—but then proceeds to do just that: describe the scene. Thus the poem ends:

> There's no way to picture it,
>   though others have often tried to.
> Here in the mountains it's like a ricochet from a sea surge,
> Meadow grass moving like sea stalks
>   in the depths of its brilliance.

Given the supposed impossibility of description, that's a pretty good shot at it. Indeed, Wright is playing with us here: persistently pointing up the limits and impossibility of description in an aw-shucks concession, then giving us four lines of verbal fireworks that light up the otherwise darkened world.

Crucial to this is Wright's diction, which is central to his poetry without being a matter of lexical range or arcane reference. Rather, it is the very play of language that opens up the world, and Wright seems to delight in stringing together "found" phrases, as *objets trouvés* waiting to be conscripted into new service. On this score, Wright is no respecter of pretensions: he moves easily from the lexicons of Dante and Rorty to country music and beer commercials. One sees this already in the title of "Hasta la Vista Buckaroo," which proceeds to explore the undoing of things "*like a rhinestone cowboy*" dissolving "[i]n a two-bit rodeo." Glen Campbell was never made so prescient, these "found" words of his now put to work in a new context. (Though, in the spirit of a kind of Appalachian Hopkins, Wright's also not averse to making up words to match the moment.)

Most often, Wright weds his descriptive power to psychological mining operations, as seen in the turns of my favorite, "The Gospel According to Yours Truly." The poem opens with a conflicted plea, a prayer verging on mockery, but is really a matter of not quite believing, though wanting to:

> Tell me again, Lord, how easy it all is—
> 　　　　　　　　　　　　renounce this,
> Renounce that, and all is a shining—
> Tell me again, I'm still here,
> 　　　　　　　　　your quick-lipped malleable boy.

Who hasn't so skeptically longed to be made anew? But our moments of resolve are so quickly dissolved by the roiling world around us. And so this turns out to be an entreaty of an Augustinian order, for chastity, but perhaps not quite yet. Looking upward to heaven, the same sky changes in an instant:

> (Strange how the clouds bump and grind, and the underthings roll,
> Strange how the grasses finger and fondle each other—
> I renounce them, I renounce them, I renounce them.
> Gnarly and thin, the nothings don't change . . .)

I don't mean to suggest that Wright is just a poetic chronicler, a lyrical photographer cataloguing the world. No, his descriptions are hallowings. They expand the mundane. The result is what's described in the very first line of the book: "The metaphysics of the quotidian" is what Wright's after, resisting the temptation to float off in metaphysical speculation, but also not content to flatten things down to the merely quotidian. This tension is held together beautifully in "Cowboy Up":

> There comes a time in one's life when one wants time,
> a lot of time, with inanimate things.
> Not ultimate inanimate things,
> Of course, but mute things,
> beautiful, untalkbackable wise things.
> That's wishful thinking, cowboy.
>
> Still, I'd like to see the river of stars
> fall noiselessly through the nine heavens for once,
> But the world's weight, and the world's welter, speak big talk and
> big confusion.

"Description," another poem intones, "is expiation." It is both "a virtual world" and "a coming to terms with"—it is both invention and response to what's given. So not only does Wright's poetry end up being doxological because of its charmed descriptions, he even offers praise *of* description, as in "Homage to What's-His-Name," which points out the lowly status of description in the pantheon of poetic moves and then, in a lightning-quick turn, reminds us that nothing comes easy:

> Ah, description, of all the arts the least appreciated.
> Well, it's just this and it's just that,
> someone will point out.
> Exactly. It's just this and it's just that and nothing other.

That poet is apocalyptic who makes us see the world in a way for the first time, and then leaves us unable to imagine how we could have seen it otherwise.

12

THE OTHER INEFFABLE

When did I start reading obituaries? I hadn't really noticed the acquisition of the habit until questioned about it by my wife. Hmmm . . . good question, dear. When *did* I start reading the obituary page? Certainly it's been since I moved to the Midwest (East and West Coasters will think such geographical exile might be reason enough to contemplate death). But I can't quite name the day or the hour, so to speak. I can't recall a moment that I was converted to obituary reading. But it is now a regular habit. (Which is not to say it's an obsession. It's not that I rush to the front porch, gather up the daily delivery, and rifle through the paper in order to seize upon the couple of pages of obituaries and memorials tucked in the back of the Region section of our city newspaper. At least not very often.)

I suppose embedded in my wife's question is a more incisive, albeit unstated one: *Why* am I reading the obituaries? I'm too young to be tracking the deaths of schoolmates

"The Other Ineffable," a review of Julian Barnes's memoir *Nothing to Be Frightened Of* (London: Jonathan Cape, 2008), first appeared in the *Harvard Divinity Bulletin* 36 (Fall 2008): 64–69. Reprinted with permission.

and old chums. I'm not even doing it to track the demise of the parents of schoolmates and old chums. I'm reading the obituaries in a foreign land: in a town not my own, in a country not my own. Because of this self-imposed exile, the names and faces staring back at me from the obituaries are not familiar to me. They are at once pages of anonymity and slices of intimacy. And yet they fascinate me, lure me, speak to me. And as my wife will attest, they leave me in tears more often than not. So why am I doing this?

Julian Barnes, cribbing from French critic Charles du Bos, would suggest that reading obituaries is perhaps my way of responding to *le réveil mortel*. Barnes thinks that a first, clunky translation of this phrase remains the best. Though "'the wake-up call to mortality' sounds a bit like a hotel service," in fact this hits just the right note: "It *is* like being in an unfamiliar hotel room, where the alarm clock has been left on the previous occupant's setting, and at some ungodly hour you are suddenly pitched from sleep into darkness, panic, and a vicious awareness that this is a rented world." *Nothing to Be Frightened Of* is Barnes's way of grappling with this wake-up call to mortality, which seems to have jarred him from his slumbers at a young age and has been harassing him ever since, as if he's been unable to change the settings on that hotel-room clock.

It is a delightfully strange book, resisting categorization much like Barnes's experimental fiction, which has often pressed "meta-fictional" questions about the relationship between history and literature (as in *A History of the World in 10½ Chapters*) or the tense relationship between art, criticism, and biography (as in *Flaubert's Parrot*). Thus he protests (a bit too much?) that this is "not my autobiography" nor can it be comprehended with recourse to "the thera-peuto-autobiographical fallacy." Instead, the book hovers somewhere between memoir, essay, and criticism. His family gets center stage, including his long-dead grandparents, his recently deceased parents, and his still-living brother, Jonathan—a philosopher of some international renown who makes regular appearances in the book as the straight-laced rationalist counterweight to Julian's "soppy" tendencies toward nostalgia. But Barnes also warns against reading *Nothing to Be Frightened Of* as a family scrapbook: "Family piety is not my motivation," he cautions.

Hence the stage is also shared by other writers, particularly French writers, mainly from the 19th century, Jules Renard in particular. (There are a few cameos by English authors like Bertrand Russell and the Austrian Wittgenstein, but none of the Germanic sources one might have expected, not even Heidegger's *Sein-zum-Tode*, which seems pretty ripe for writerly musing.) At times it feels as if the book began its life on index cards filled with quotes and passages from these writers, which the author has now taken up, not just as a foil, but because they have given him words to try to grapple with *le réveil mortel*—which amounts to a veritable gauntlet that death throws down at the writer's feet. At one point he castigates himself for failing in the face of this challenge:

> Only a couple of nights ago, there came again that alarmed and alarming moment, of being pitch-forked back into consciousness, awake, alone, utterly alone, beating pillow with fist shouting "oh no Oh No OH NO" in an endless wail, the horror of the

moment—the minutes—overwhelming what might, to an objective witness, appear a shocking display of self-exhibitionist pity. An inarticulate one, too: for what sometimes shames me is the extraordinary lack of descriptive, or responsive, words that come out of my mouth. For God's sake, you're a *writer*, I say to myself. You do *words*. Can't you improve on that? Can't you face down death—well, you won't ever face it down, but can't you at least protest against it—more interestingly than this? (p. 126)

Barnes himself has suggested that it was Flaubert who found a language for sex; Edmund Wilson claimed that D. H. Lawrence finally found an English vocabulary for the same. We might suggest that Barnes has written a book that picks up the gauntlet, hoping to find a language for death. That language is crisp, even breezy; Barnes doesn't impress (or intimidate) his readers by scouring the *OED* for arcane expressions. His prose has a cunning simplicity about it that feels incredibly honest—honest enough to sometimes be vulgar, at other times sentimental. One might say that in his hands the language of death is democratic—which makes good sense since death is quite impartial (talk about *e pluribus unum!*). And, as one would expect from Barnes, the language of death also turns out to be funny as hell.

The Un-memoir

While *Nothing to Be Frightened Of* is not straightforwardly an autobiography, memoir, or an essay, its own slipperiness continues Barnes's pursuit of some of those slippery differences and distinctions that get put into question by what we call "metareflections." Here the persistent theme is the unreliability of memory, and hence the very fuzziness of the genres of autobiography and memoir, not to mention history and legal testimony (better addressed in the "fiction" of *A History of the World*). The theme is introduced in a banal way just as we are also meeting his family, including his grandparents who would sometimes entertain themselves with a ritual the grandchildren called "The Reading of the Diaries." Having kept separate diaries, Grandma and Grandpa would read their entries for the same day, but several years prior. Grandpa's entry would read: "Friday. Worked in garden. Planted potatoes." "Nonsense," Grandma would retort, reading her entry for the very same day: "Rained all day. Too wet to work in garden." Here the elusive nature of the description, not to mention memory, makes itself felt. This is at least part of the reason we have four Gospels.

Unlike his philosopher brother who distrusts memories, at least early on Barnes the novelist only distrusts "the way we color them in." This basic trust of memory is corroborated by an archive: "I also have the family documentation in the shallow drawer to back me up." But by the end of the book it seems as if this basic, albeit chastened, trust of memory has begun to tremble a bit, on the verge of crumbling, along with prior tidy distinctions between fiction and history or art and criticism. And not even an archive of documentation will save it. Indeed, in the case of Stendhal's famous bout of "Stendhal Syndrome" in Florence, the archive dismantles the memory: what is recounted by Henri Stendhal in 1826 has almost no connection to what was recorded in the journals of (then) Henri Beyle in 1811. "Memory took one road," Barnes comments, "and truth another." Not even the eyewitness testimony of Barnes's young nieces regarding a childhood story told by his brother holds up. Instead he gets three conflicting accounts of the same event. "You see (again) why (in part) I am a novelist?" The result is that "memory itself comes to seem much closer to an act of the imagination than ever before."

But this is still not a distrust of memory; it is, instead, an appreciation for "different kinds of truthfulness." Indeed, Barnes seems to find in this the very vocation of the novelist: "I am left with a new proposed definition of what I do: a novelist is someone who remembers nothing yet records and manipulates different versions of what he doesn't remember." So the novelist, he concludes, "is less interested in the exact nature of that truth, more in the nature of the believers, the manner in which they hold their beliefs, and the texture of the ground between competing narratives." That could also pass as a pretty good description of a theologian.

A Religion Worth (Not) Believing

"I don't believe in God, but I miss Him." This is the opening line of the book, described by the author's philosopher brother as "soppy." Despite being solidly secular in a way that must still seem exotic to many Americans ("I was never baptized, never sent to Sunday school. I have never been to a normal church service in my life"), Barnes does not offer merely secularized meditations on death. Questions in the orbit of death and extinction inevitably raise questions about eternity and the afterlife, till pretty soon you find yourself bumping up against questions about God and divinity. Barnes follows the questions where they might lead, and shows an understanding of some of the nuances of Christianity that are missed by others in his generation. (This stems at least in part from time spent in France teaching at a Catholic school.)

That's not to say he isn't up-front about his agnosticism. As part of an inverse hagiography, Barnes shows an interest in conversions to atheism and agnosticism, querying his family and friends regarding when and how they lost their faith (not unlike new evangelical friends who are interested in when I became a Christian—by which they mean, *date* and *time*, please). Barnes's own testimony in this regard is entirely adolescent and completely honest:

> My own final letting go of the remnant, or possibility, of religion, happened at a later age. As an adolescent, hunched over some book or magazine in the family bathroom, I used to tell myself that God couldn't possibly exist because the notion that He might be watching me while I masturbated was absurd; even more absurd was the notion that all my dead ancestors might be lined up and watching too. . . . The thought of Grandma and Grandpa observing what I was up to would have seriously put me off my stroke. (p. 14)

No evidential problem of evil; no intellectual dissatisfaction with the doctrine of the incarnation; no vaulted claims to rational enlightenment; just an honest, onanistic confession of a rather pragmatic agnosticism. But more titillating, in fact, is Barnes's mature reflection on this loss of faith:

> As I record this now, however, I wonder why I didn't think through more of the possibilities. Why did I assume that God, if He *was* watching, necessarily disapproved of how I was spilling my seed? Why did it not occur to me that if the sky did not fall in as it witnessed my zealous and unflagging self-abuse, this might be because the sky did not judge it a sin? Nor did I have the imagination to conceive of my dead ancestors equally smiling on my actions: go on, my son, enjoy it while you've got it, there won't be much more of that once you're a disembodied spirit, so have another one for us. (pp. 14-15)

He thus owns up to his "breezy illogic" in moments of self-critique, and the critique of others who lost faith in God because of unanswered prayers: "No subsequent reflection from any of us that perhaps God's main business, were He to exist, might not be as an adolescent helpline, goods-provider, or masturbation-scourge. No, out with Him once and for all."

Unlike so many secularist screeds that are happy to caricature religion whenever possible, Barnes resists such easy targets. But he also resists defanging religion. Indeed, the agnostic Barnes can sometimes be a surprising apologist for what might be construed as conservative religion. Intolerant with squishy spirituality, he finds "the notion of redefining the deity into something that works for you" as nothing short of "grotesque." Recounting a dinner party with neighbors, he overheard a young man shout sarcastically, "But why should God do that for His son and not for the rest of us?" "Because He's *God*, for Christ's sake," Barnes shouted back. Taking up the mantle of agnostic prophet, he hurls criticism at the idolatries of "C of E" (Church of England) niceties, in a way that surprisingly echoes Cardinal Newman's famous critique of "Liberalism": "There seems little point," Barnes muses, "in a religion which is merely a weekly social event (apart, of course, from the normal pleasures of a weekly social event), as opposed to one which tells you exactly how to live, which colours and stains everything." The metaphor returns later: "What's the point of faith unless you and it are serious—*seriously* serious—unless your religion fills, directs, stains and sustains your life?" If the young Barnes thought a God who cared about stains on his trousers couldn't possibly exist, the older Barnes thinks the only religion worth embracing (and rejecting) is one that stains everything.

Doubting Disbelief

It's hard not to read *Nothing to Be Frightened Of* against the backdrop of "new atheist" bestsellers by Dawkins, Dennett, Harris, and Hitchens. But Julian Barnes will not be anthologized in the next edition of Christopher Hitchens's *Portable Atheist* (which just barely masks its desire to be the Hitchens Bible; I'm holding out for the Hitchens Atheist Study Bible, with evolutionary charts and all). Unlike Ian McEwan and Salman Rushdie (literary figures with their own epistles in Hitchens's canon), Barnes lacks the fundamentalist swagger of the new atheists. In particular, he lacks their chronological snobbery and their epistemological confidence:

If I called myself an atheist at twenty, and an agnostic at fifty and sixty, it isn't because I've acquired more knowledge in the meantime: just more awareness of ignorance. How can we be sure that we know enough to know? As twenty-first century neo-Darwinian materialists, convinced that the meaning and mechanism of life have only been fully clear since the year 1859, we hold ourselves categorically wiser than those credulous knee-benders who, a speck of time away, believed in divine purpose, an ordered world, resurrection and a Last Judgement. But although we are more informed, we are no more evolved, and certainly no more intelligent than them. What convinces us our knowledge is so final? (p. 22)

Given his own epistemological tentativeness, Barnes can't resist a bit of fun, imagining a divine game at the expense of our celebrity atheists:

If there were a games-playing God, He would surely get especial ludic pleasure from disappointing those philosophers who had convinced themselves and others of His non-existence. A. J. Ayer assures Somerset Maugham that there is nothing, and nothingness, after death: whereupon they both find themselves players in God's little end-of-the-pier entertainment called Watch the Fury of the Resurrected Atheist. That's a neat would-you-rather for the God-denying philosopher: would you rather there was nothing after death, and you were proved right, or that there was a wonderful surprise, and your professional reputation was destroyed? (pp. 212–13)

In short, Barnes has nothing to do with the silliness that claims that "religion poisons everything." To the contrary, Barnes's appreciation for religious art—both painting and music—is one of the best sections of the book, and leaves him not a little haunted. "Missing God is focused for me," he confesses, "by missing the underlying sense of purpose and belief when confronted with religious art." He seems, if not tempted, at least a bit intrigued by an *aesthetic* argument never entertained in Aquinas's "Five Ways": that it might just be true because it is beautiful. "The Christian religion didn't last so long merely because everyone believed it," Barnes observes. It lasted because it makes for a helluva novel—which is pretty close to Tolkien's claim that the gospel is true because it is the most fantastic fantasy, the greatest fairy story ever told. And Barnes, a great lover of both music and painting, knows that much of what he enjoys owes its existence to Christianity. Without the madness of the gospel, Mozart would never have composed a requiem, Giotto would never have left us the treasures in the chapel of Padua. Thus he finds himself asking, "What if it were true?"—a question never entertained by the dogmaticians of the new atheism. What would it be like, he asks, to listen to Mozart's *Requiem* and take it as nonfiction?

Unfortunately, at this point Barnes constructs a false dichotomy: "The Christian," he surmises, "would . . . have been concerned more with truth than aesthetics." Whence the distinction? One might say that the madness of the incarnation obliterates such a dichotomy, that the logic of incarnation scandalously claims that truth and beauty kiss (cf. Ps. 85:10). Taking it to be true does not trump the beauty; receiving it as nonfiction does not de-aestheticize the work of art, reducing it to a textbook. But though Barnes's dichotomy is misplaced, it seems laudable that he entertains what it would mean for these works of art to also be *more* than (merely) aesthetic. "It is one of the haunting hypotheticals for the non-believer," he concludes: "What would it be like 'if it were true?'"

In this openness to haunting, Barnes remains a good disciple of Flaubert, on whom he comments:

> While he distrusted religions, he had a tenderness towards the spiritual impulse, and was suspicious of militant atheism. "Each dogma in itself is repulsive to me," he wrote. "But I consider the feeling that engendered them to be the most natural and poetic expression of humanity. I don't like those philosophers who have dismissed it as foolishness and humbug. What I find there is necessity and instinct. So I respect the black man kissing his fetish as much as I do the Catholic kneeling before the Sacred Heart." (p. 176)

It is Barnes's *flaubertien* self-suspicion that I find both interesting and winsome—not because I think it provides comfort or fodder for my faith, but because it illustrates the possibility of being an atheist without being a fundamentalist. It also strikes me as something many believers would do well to imitate.

13

THE INCARNATION IS LOCAL

I was chaining my bike outside Literary Life, our local treasure of an independent bookstore, and was delighted to run
into Rick and Brenda Beerhorst, our resident neighborhood
artists and activists who have been catalysts for redemption
and joy right here in the southeast corner of Grand Rapids,
Michigan. We were all there to enjoy a reading from a local
poet who was unfamiliar to me. Rick, with a hint of des-
peration in his voice, was leaving a series of messages for
a friend, John, but I was eager to get inside for the reading,
which was to begin at any moment. Just before excusing
myself, a wiry, somewhat gnarled character made his way
up the sidewalk, his white t-shirt a mess of dirt and oil. Rick
seemed to sigh in relief: "Where have you been?" he asked,
perplexed and just a little perturbed. And pretty soon I realized I didn't have to rush into the reading: here was our
poet, John Rybicki.

This image of the poet-as-auto-mechanic is indelibly

This essay first appeared as "The Incarnation is Local: The Poetry of John
Rybicki" at *Comment* online (December 31, 2010). Reprinted with permission.

inscribed in my mind when I think of the work of John Rybicki. Indeed, it is the perfect context in which to hear him,
for the connection and contradiction are embedded in his
oeuvre as well. Consider, for example, "Tire Shop Poem," in
his marvelous collection *We Bed Down Into Water* (whose
cover is graced with a Rick Beerhorst engraving). The poem
ends with a flourish of lyrical delight that pulls holiness
from the middle of the workaday, finding the music in the
mundane (do yourself a favor and read this out loud):

> I catch his dare and rubber roll
> a tire up my calf and pop
>
> the center cap, clamp and spin,
> hammer lead weights onto rim
>
> after dizzying rim. I lug nut smash
> and flick the pry bar from one hand
>
> to the next. Fred Astaire in a
> tire shop, where we slap our boots
>
> across all that slop to outdistance
> fire, outdistance that burning bush
>
> that follows us everywhere.

I say "contradiction" but should perhaps speak of "par-
adoxes" or "productive tensions"—the way catgut strings
pulled taut by opposing forces can generate a Bach cantata.
This collection and his most recent work are riven by his
wife's cancer, torn between lament and eulogy, resistance
and dependence. This dynamic was stunningly present in a
new poem he shared that evening, "On a Piece of Paper You
Were About to Burn." Overwhelmed by it, I half staggered

to John afterward to thank him, and he graciously passed along the crumpled copy to me. On it were the words to a poem written in the wake, not of his wife Julie's illness, but of her death. And the second-person address won't let us escape the sorrow.

> How do you hold the dead
> when they're hammered into a room
> so flat you can pick your teeth
>
> with one corner of the picture? When you were the one
> at that moment aiming the cheap camera at her
> wanting to fold her light
>
> into a square locket of time.

The poet recounts how the photo brings to mind the background music playing at the moment of the aperture's capture: the Dixie Chicks' "Cowboy, Take Me Away."

> But now that she's a crumb inside the earth,
>
> the song punches little whispery nail holes
> in the bottom of your boat.

An entire world has been reduced to this, flattened and frozen in this cramped frame. And then the poet, putting us right there in that "you," names exactly how we'd expect to find ourselves in the wake of such a loss:

> You rock on the kitchen floor hugging your own legs,
> weeping and kissing a face so tiny
> you could cover it with a penny.

> You repeat the same prayer to her over and over,
> as if your heart were the governor on death's engine.
> How could God smash a room flat into a photo
>
> and do it over and over again?

But Rybicki doesn't ensconce himself in sadness; indeed, romance regularly reveals itself. What's so heartbreakingly remarkable is how many of these poems of lament and protest break into love songs without falling prey to the self-help drivel that besets our death-denying culture. In "Me and My Lass, We Are a Poem," constantly haunted by his wife's mortality, Rybicki somehow hymns their love without hiding from death.

> When we lie down in the earth,
> we'll need coffins with holes bored
>
> through their sides: we'll each have
> one arm hanging out
>
> so I can take hold of her
> hand, even while we're in the dirt.

It is a sign of Rybicki's provocation that I find myself asking, is every lament a backhanded longing for love?

But I don't mean to reduce Rybicki's genius to his themes. Space (and copyright law) leave me only pleading with the reader to go find Rybicki and read him whole, for the real enchantment of his poetry is the almost surreal play of words and sounds that can only be appreciated out loud. Those who like their poetry straight-up and prosaic will be a bit frustrated, but who can fail to sit on the edge of their linguistic seat when he opens "A Song for Kay Mullen" with fantasias like this:

The flaming balls float when our hands
    are busy elsewhere.
Juggling's easy: first, study hypnosis
    and rock your finger
metronome in front of a cross
    on the highway. Go back
to that day when one alphabet devoured
    another. You have two animals
with their brights on, their eyes following
    the ticktock rock of your finger,
so the cross with the dusty flowers
    around its neck evaporates
under a mother's pillow.

This is poetry for tongues and ears, not just minds.

When Rick and Brenda eventually escorted John into the bookstore, they rustled up a clean t-shirt from somewhere and pushed him up to the front where we all waited quietly to hear his poetry. John launched into a lyrical apology laced with passion and pain. I thought to myself, "Wow, he's doing this poem from memory" and then realized that this wasn't a poem—this was just John talking. The delights of his poetry were only intensified in his everyday speech. And it struck me that this embodied a lesson I learned that day: the delights of art are not sequestered in Manhattan or Los Angeles. The aesthetic is not the property of the cosmopolitan. To the contrary, the arts are alive and well in neighborhoods that never get noticed by the *New York Times* or *Art in America*—in local collectives of provincial laborers who are creating works of praise and lament right around the corner while we pine away, feeling sorry for ourselves because we're stuck in some Midwest town, longingly reading the *New Yorker*.

I'm reminded of Eugene Peterson's whimsical translation of John 1:14 in *The Message*: "The Word became flesh and blood and moved into the neighborhood." Those of us who take special delight in the arts, grateful for the multitudinous gifts of our Creator, might adopt the same incarnational approach and be looking for artistic treasures right in the neighborhood.

14

Erotic Theology

Contemporary theology is a lot of things, but "poetic" it is not. Quite the contrary: long captivated by the supposed rigor of a flattened rationalism, and saddled with a desire for intellectual respectability, theology speaks in the jargon-laden tongue of the academy. In the name of analytic precision and conceptual clarity, contemporary theologians approach metaphor like Saint George meets the dragon: as an enemy to be vanquished by the lance of univocity. This situation is both tragic and ironic: tragic that discourse about the Creator could be so unimaginative and dull, and ironic that speech about the incarnate God should have so little room for mystery.

Hence my eagerness upon seeing William Dyrness's new volume, *Poetic Theology*. As one who plies his trade in theology but spends his evenings curled up with poetry, Dyrness's project sounded a peal of hope for me—here, finally, is someone returning theology to its proper home in

"Erotic Theology," a review of William A. Dyrness, *Poetic Theology: God and the Poetics of Everyday Life* (Grand Rapids, MI: Eerdmans, 2011), first appeared in *Image: A Journal of Arts & Religion* 69 (May 2011): 70–72.

a language more befitting the Word become flesh. And the opening page of *Poetic Theology* is a tease in precisely that direction, promising to connect poetry and theology, albeit in "the pigeon-toed prose of theology—a dog barking at the moon" (p. ix). A metaphor on the first page: the theologian as baying canine. Not exactly Dante, but we'll take what we can get; this holds promise.

Unfortunately, the book I wanted—and the book Dyrness seemed to promise in that opening paragraph—is different from the book he has written. Take a moment or two to work through that (it took me quite a bit longer), and we'll be in a position to then receive the book for what it is: a theological affirmation of the arts and "everyday poetics" as expressions of human nature's ineradicable longings. It is an *apologia* for theology to take seriously all sorts of human making (*poiēsis*), especially artistic creation, precisely because our culture-making efforts express the core of human being: our loves, our longings, our desires.

It takes a while for Dyrness to come clean on this, mainly because the opening section includes a constellation of concepts that he treats as roughly synonymous, whereas others might parse them as more distinct. For example, while he opens by talking about the "poetic" in relation to poetry, already on the second page it becomes clear that the force of the poetic here is more etymological: Dyrness is interested in *making*, in cultural labor more generally, in the cultivation of creative possibilities. Other terms blink in and out of this constellation: the aesthetic, the symbolic, the imaginative, the beautiful. These seem to be treated as either roughly synonymous or at least significantly overlapping, which I found to be both confusing and frustrating.

But all of this finally crystallizes when Dyrness hits his Augustinian stride and we realize his primary quarry: desire. "Whether this is recognized or not," he concludes, behind our cultural projects

> lies Augustine's notion that the self is defined not by what it knows but by what it sees and loves. Although ignorant of its source, and confessedly non-creedal, postmodern people are radically committed to this Augustinian creed. They are living examples of the medieval adage: You become what you behold. Just look at a typical football fan on a Saturday afternoon, or a groupie during a rock concert. The modern person's life is defined, often unconsciously, by what they contemplate—the vision of what they indwell in affirmation and affection. (p. 201)

Now the constellation crystallizes into shape: it is precisely because desire is operative on a register that is more imaginative than intellectual—more attuned to beauty than deduction, more activated by the symbolic than the conceptual—that Dyrness's theological account of human desire must also attend to the aesthetic. Given this, one might suggest that the book would have been better titled *Erotic Theology*.

But I've still only sketched half of his project: a "poetic" theology is a theology attuned to desire, and to the expression of our longings in cultural artifacts. But Dyrness also regularly describes his project as an "apologetic." What could this mean? If he's concerned with beauty, aesthetics, and symbolism, we're obviously a long way from the flat-footed demonstrations of *Evidence That Demands a*

Verdict. So what does it mean to describe this poetic theology as "apologetic?"

It seems to me the term operates in two ways: first, Dyrness is mounting a defense—an *apologia*—of cultural production as a site for our most basic longings and desires, and thus as a prime topic for theological reflection. In other words, he's trying to convince theologians to pay attention to more than ideas, beliefs, and doctrines—to be attuned to culture's "making" as some of the most potent expressions of our love, especially since (according to Augustine) it is our love that truly defines us. On this score, Dyrness's apologetic is directed to those theologians who write as if human beings were primarily thinking things untainted by cultural context—as if humans (even theologians) didn't inhabit a symbolic world in which they are more moved than convinced, more subject to the dynamics of attraction than deduction. Let's stop writing theology for brains on a stick, Dyrness is saying, to which I can only add my "Amen."

But there is a second, more charged, aspect to his apologetic: Dyrness wants us to be attentive to the longings expressed in cultural production precisely because of their *religious* significance. Poetic theology, he concludes, "suggests that the Christian faith, and consonant human flourishing, are to be shaped in part by embracing the play of light and love that is to be found in the wisdom of the surrounding culture—what sparks affection in its objects, patterns, and tales" (p. 285). Thus poetic theology "seeks to do a religious reading of these deep-seated cultural longings. For these longings, insofar as they reflect the goodness of the created order and God's loving presence there, constitute a partial vision of God" (p. 286).

It is precisely this second aspect of the apologetic where I would demur from the emphases of Dyrness's project. While I think Dyrness is exactly right to honor the fundamentally *religious* impulses that characterize our longings (and hence the arts), he tends to thereby read them as implicitly theistic, even anonymously Christian—as if they're on the right track but just don't quite get to their target, often because they don't realize what they're really intending. Thus Dyrness claims that "post-Romantic people are *already engaged* in practices that spark affection and move them toward a vision of a good life" even if they "may not see" that these refer to a transcendent God (p. 211; emphasis original). But one could worry that this is a bit of a colonizing move. While Dyrness argues that "all good art, . . . even against its will, echoes this reality" (p. 247), I wonder just how secular artists would welcome the claim that their art is really longing for God. There's a way to make that point, but Dyrness doesn't quite make it. We've all heard the quip, often (mis)attributed to Chesterton, that a man knocking on the door of a brothel actually desires God. Indeed, Graham Greene's *Heart of the Matter* is an extended meditation on the idea. But surely that doesn't entail affirming that lust is an inchoate worship and stunted praise, even if the persistence of such longing is itself a testament to our nature. (I have discussed these dynamics in Greene, Walker Percy, and Evelyn Waugh in my *Desiring the Kingdom*.)

There is a further problematic consequence of his move: unwittingly, Dyrness often ends up instrumentalizing art. His reading of cultural artifacts turns out to be another "finding God" project: the arts are affirmed insofar as they "can move people toward God" (p. 92). This finds expression in the structure of the book, which culminates by focusing on the role of art in worship—a much-welcomed and much-needed emphasis, but one that also fuels the worry about instrumentalization. Perhaps unwittingly, the apologetic aspect of Dyrness's affirmation ends up with only a qualified affirmation of the arts, unable to affirm arts that unpack the world even if they have no aspiration toward transcendence.

Dyrness is right to build an apologetic on the basis of our longings, and he's exactly right that Augustine would read these cultural longings as a testament to our nature as desiring creatures. But Augustine would not thereby affirm them as rightly ordered "as far as they go"; rather, Augustine would emphasize that even *dis*-ordered love is still a backhanded witness to our nature, that God has made us for himself and that our hearts are restless until they rest in him. That doesn't mean that our disordered longings merely fall short; they are aimed in the wrong direction. What makes these religious is not that they are almost Christian, but rather that they are idolatrous. But for Augustine, even idolatry is a witness, and even the "splendid vices" of Rome are not without their virtues. As Jean-Luc Marion has said, idolatry is its own "low-water mark" of divine revelation. We don't need to thereby make idolatry a tepid theism to prefer it over naturalism.

Dyrness has written an impassioned apologetic for the arts—one that will be especially important for those recovering from the latent Gnosticism of so much of evangelicalism. But I'm still trying to get over that opening page which birthed in me a longing for a genre that remains to be realized: a poetic theology.

Part

4

LINES
OF SIGHT
Thinking in Context

S EVERAL YEARS AGO, A CREW OF ART AND DESIGN STU-
dents from the Kendall College of Art and Design in
Grand Rapids staged a "site lab" exhibit. The project was
both innovative and adaptive, creative and redemptive. They
took over a long-abandoned art deco building at the very
heart of the city, sitting on the corner of Fulton Street and
Division Avenue. The art students imagined the shell of a
building that had lain derelict for a decade as an unwitting
gallery or exhibit hall, just waiting to be filled. They then
commissioned a wide array of site-specific works, generated to custom-fit the space—working with its contours,
responding to its challenges, utilizing its unique gifts and
resources. The result was a stunning exhibition indexed to
a specific time and place, but with a value that transcended
those specifics.

You might think of the chapters in this section as site-
specific. They are occasioned by specific issues and challenges, and often by specific invitations and questions, but

call for analysis and reflection that transcends their situation. Sometimes these include from-the-hip responses to current events or above-the-fold urgencies—which is also why sometimes such writing is brief, compressed, dashed off to interject in the moment. In other cases, such site-specific interventions call for teasing out implications, finding "lines of sight" to read a situation or tackle a problem. The result, I hope is a series of context-specific meditations that bear value beyond their original locations.

15

DREAM SMALL

*Catch for us the foxes, the little foxes that ruin the vineyards,
our vineyards that are in bloom.* (Song of Songs 2:15)

Mr. President, Esteemed Faculty, Family and Friends of the graduates, and, most importantly, Graduating Class of 2011,

I'm guessing the faculty and admission counselors of this fine institution lured you here with some hefty promises and big talk—that a King College education would equip you to transform culture, turn the world upside down, and become leaders in your field, all while roller skating backwards, juggling flaming chainsaws, and battling poverty in rural Alabama! (Been there, done that.) On the way in here, you were encouraged to "dream big."

On your way out there I have a different exhortation for you: **"Dream *small.*"**

Now I want you to understand that exhortation. I'm not

This was first shared as a commencement address to the class of 2011 at King College in Bristol, TN. I'm grateful to Dale Brown, director of the Buechner Institute, for both the invitation and his hospitality. I might also note that their athletic teams compete as the King College Tornado.

suggesting you shouldn't dream big. And without question, your King College education has well equipped you to do whatever God might be calling you to in his broken-but-blessed world—to be a veritable Tornado of grace and accomplishment, cutting a swath through this world that will leave behind a wake of compassion and achievement.

So I have every expectation that you will continue to dream big. Indeed, I think that all comes rather naturally for us. We inhabit a culture that resounds with messages and covert rituals that all subtly encourage us to pursue the bigger, the better, the mega. Even the church has been emboldened of late with big plans for transforming culture, newly confident in our ability to redeem the world. You have been told your whole life that you can do whatever you put your mind to. So "dreaming big" has sort of become second nature for us. We are so constantly expanding our horizons, enlarging our territories, and looking toward a bright, shiny future of accomplishment that it's hard for us to see all the little stuff right in front of us.

So you don't need me to tell you to dream big. But I do hope you'll hear me when I encourage you to also dream small. Because that might be what really matters. And it might be where your education really pays off.

The Little Foxes

There is a curious little passage buried in the Song of Solomon that is germane to this point. (If you know your Bible, and you know the Song of Solomon, then you're now hoping I'm going to talk about sex. I'll see what I can do.) The poetry invokes a concern with the little things through a viticultural metaphor of fruit bearing. It goes like this: "Catch for us the foxes, the little foxes that ruin the vineyards, our vineyards that are in bloom" (Song of Songs 2:15).

It's the little foxes the ruin the vineyard. If you're always dreaming big—surveying your vineyard, plotting the next acquisition of the vineyard down the road, dreaming about all your plans for the estate—in other words, if you tend to always look beyond the vineyard and don't enjoy actually caring for the vines, you'll miss the pesky little foxes that are ruining what's right in front of you. You'll never be able to enjoy the wine of the vineyard if you ignore the little foxes. You won't enjoy the fruit of the vine if you don't tend to the nitty-gritty, down-and-dirty work of viticulture.

And here's what you might not yet realize: that real joy is found right there in the dirt, in the ho-hum task of tending the plant, in cultivating the *terroir* that will nourish the vines that yield the fruit. While you're imagining all of the outcomes of the vineyard and all the benefits to be reaped, what might be hard for you to imagine is that some of your best days—when you feel like all is right with the universe and what you're doing *means* something and you know why you're here and your heart swells in gratitude and joy—well, those will be days when you're mucking about in the vineyard, tending to the little foxes.

All right, let's come back from the metaphor for a minute. Please don't hear this as some moralism about the necessity for hard work so that you can enjoy a big payoff. This isn't some literary version of the no-pain, no-gain gospel of accomplishment and "success." To the contrary, what I'm suggesting is this: so many of the big dreams that you now envision as "success" are going to feel unbelievably empty and vapid and anticlimactic when you get there. In fact, let me put it starkly: if you keep thinking happiness is in the land of big dreams, then you are on a trajectory toward disappointment. If you only dream big, you're headed for disillusionment—not because you can't do it, but precisely because you *can*! We're sending you out of here with the ticket to success. But it can be just that "success" that will feel hollow and deflated unless you learn to dream small.

Talk to all kinds of people who have achieved everything they set out to do in this life, who made it to the top of their professional heap, and what you'll often hear is this: "It's not what I thought it would be." What it turns out to be, even at the height of accomplishment, is boring as hell. Just when you've spent a life climbing to that fabled "top," where you thought having it all would mean everything, you get there only to discover that it doesn't mean all that much. This is why tedium and ennui are the demons of modernity. And the only way to exorcise them is with gratitude for the mundane. The bacchanalian delights of the wine are going to have diminishing returns; you need to find joy in actually tending the vineyard, in concern for "the little foxes."

Here a parable comes to mind: the parable of Lester Burnham as told in the film *American Beauty*. You might recall Lester, played so well by Kevin Spacey, mired in the boredom and placid emptiness of what was supposed to be a "successful" American life. He is finally awoken from his suburban slumber by *fantasizing* about Angela, who he thinks is the girl of his dreams (his wife Carolyn notwithstanding!). So Lester falls into the trap of thinking that happiness is to be found in the fantastic, in a dream-world that is something other than his mundane, workaday existence.

But just when he is about to attain his dream, he realizes that what he's wanted has been right in front of him this whole time. It's just that his fantasies and dreams blinded him to all the delights enfolded in his own little world. And so the film closes with this moving, post-mortem soliloquy:

> I had always heard your entire life flashes in front of your eyes the second before you die. First of all, that one second isn't a second at all, it stretches on forever, like an ocean of time . . . For me, it was lying on my back at Boy Scout camp, watching falling stars . . . And yellow leaves, from the maple trees, that lined our street . . . Or my grandmother's hands, and the way her skin seemed like paper . . . And the first time I saw my cousin Tony's brand new Firebird . . . And Janie . . . And Janie . . . And . . . Carolyn.
>
> I guess I could be pretty pissed off about what happened to me . . . but it's hard to stay mad, when there's so much beauty in the world. Sometimes I feel like I'm seeing it all at once, and it's too much, and my heart fills up like a balloon that's about to burst . . . And then I remember to relax, and stop trying to hold on to it, and then it flows through me like rain and I can't feel anything but gratitude for every single moment of my stupid little life . . . You have no idea what I'm talking about, I'm sure. But don't worry . . . you will someday.

Graduates, I'm trying to plant a little seed that can sprout for you on that "someday."

Learning to Love

The measure of your education is not what you know, but what you *love*. And as Saint Augustine never tired of saying, what you love is what you *enjoy*. Your teachers have not just tried to inform you about the world; they've tried to pass on to you a love for corners of God's world that you perhaps never saw before. They have invited you into the nooks and crannies of God's creation—into the fascinating complexity of the brain or the mournful cadences of Bach, in the play of poetry or the dazzle of digital media. You've been invited to wonder, to be perplexed, to puzzle, to discern, to critique, to take delight. To *enjoy*. Your education hasn't just equipped you for a career, it has trained your joy.

Hopefully your education here at King has plucked strings you didn't even know you had, activated parts of you that were dormant. In short, I hope your education has expanded your very self because it has taught you to love new things and find joy and meaning right in front of you. Because it is precisely that capacity that will enable you to dream small—to bloom and flourish in the everyday. It is precisely the baptized curiosity of a full-orbed Christian education—reflected in the core curriculum at the heart of your King degree—that will enable you to resist both the fantasy of big-dream happiness as well as the numbness and tedium of late modern life. Your education has taught you how to care about what really matters because it has equipped you to see the world with new eyes, to engage the world with new commitments, to redeem the world with renewed passion. And you can do that wherever you are. This sort of holistic education deepens the mundane and enriches the quotidian—it enchants the everyday. Believe me, you're going to need that.

You have been entrusted with a gift; you are now a steward of your education. What will you do with it? Dreaming big is easy. The bigger challenge is to dream small—to draw on the gift of your education to deepen your embeddedness in the gritty realities of everyday life. Your education has equipped you to take on the world; but I want you to realize that it has also equipped you to pay attention to the little foxes.

Do you have grand visions of transforming the world economy? Fantastic. How about you start by moving to "the abandoned spaces of empire"[1]—committing to live day in and day out in the vicinity of those who are crushed underfoot by existing economic systems. Your education has taught you why that is important and how it can be meaningful. Can you dream small enough that you can find joy and significance in the texture of a neighborhood? Are you willing to follow our incarnating God who also dreamed small—who, when he came to dwell in the neighborhood of humanity, did not relocate to Rome but moved to the other side of the tracks in tiny Nazareth?

Or do you fantasize about being the next social media guru, imagining hitherto-unthought-of ways to connect the world by digital links? Marvelous. Just don't forget to build friendships and relationships with people who have bodies, who are close by, who will sit with you in valleys and drink with you on the mountaintops of your experience. Don't forget the hard good work of being part of a congregation that worships God and feeds the poor, despite the fact that it frustrates you to no end. Don't forget the hard good work of building marriages and families that are little microcosms of the coming kingdom; it will be the hardest and the best thing you'll ever do.

Because it's in these mundane, workaday spaces that you'll find a meaning and a hope and a joy that endures. I know you're dreaming big dreams. I know you're already imagining the heights you'll scale. Please do. I just want you to know that if you can also marshal the ability to dream small, you'll find what you're looking for in the most unexpected places. In fact, let me close with a poem by Todd Boss, who bears witness to this sort of mundane revelation.

This Morning in a Morning Voice

to beat the froggiest
of morning voices,
  my son gets out of bed
and takes a lumpish song
  along—a little lyric
learned in kindergarten,
  something about a
boat. He's found it in
  the bog of his throat
before his feet have hit
  the ground, follows
its wonky melody down
  the hall and into the loo
as if it were the most
  natural thing for a little
boy to do, and lets it
  loose awhile in there
to a tinkling sound while
  I lie still in bed, alive
like I've never been, in
  love again with life,
afraid they'll find me
  drowned here, drowned
in more than my fair
  share of joy.[2]

Class of 2011: May God bless you with the same.

Notes

1. Rutba House, *School(s) for Conversion: 12 Marks of a New Monasticism* (Eugene, OR: Wipf & Stock, 2005), pp. 10ff.
2. "This Morning in a Morning Voice," from pitch: poems by Todd Boss. Copyright © 2012 by Todd Boss. Used by permission of W. W. Norton & Company, Inc.

16

WHAT'S RIGHT WITH THE PROSPERITY GOSPEL?

An Economy of Abundance

In contrast to the logic of scarcity with which we are all too familiar, Walter Brueggemann put his finger on the pulse of God's economy by describing it as a "liturgy of abundance." God's economy, he pointed out, assumes the plenitude of creation and thus refuses the miserly hoarding and competition yielded by the myth of scarcity. It's Pharoah's logic, he suggested, that generates an economy of fear: "There's not enough. Let's get everything."[1] In contrast, Jesus came to demonstrate an extravagant, wonder-working economy that makes wine out of water. In this economy of abundance, not only is there enough fish and bread to go around, there are baskets and baskets left over (John 6:11–13). God's profligate creating and re-creating almost borders on being wasteful.

Not surprisingly, then, some have seized upon John

"What's Right with the Prosperity Gospel?," *Calvin Theological Seminary Forum* 16 (Fall 2009): 8–9. Reprinted with permission.

10:10 as central to the gospel, where Jesus announces: "I came that they may have life, and have it *abundantly*."

From Abundance to Prosperity

Unfortunately, this promise of abundant life is often taken up by those we identify with the "prosperity gospel": a gospel of "health and wealth" associated with folks like Joel Osteen of Lakewood Church is Houston, Texas, or Creflo Dollar's World Changers Church outside Atlanta. You might be familiar with its slogans, plucked from Scripture:

- "You have not because you ask not." (a common paraphrase of James 4:2)
- "Ask and you will receive." (John 16:24)
- Jesus came "that [you] may have life, and have it *abundantly*." (John 10:10)

This seems to resonate with creation's economy of abundance. Wouldn't an economy of abundance be one that generates *prosperity*?

And yet I'm guessing most of us would squirm (or scream) if we had to watch the Trinity Broadcasting Network for any extended amount of time. Many of us would cringe to see Creflo Dollar positioning the Cadillac Escalade beside his pulpit as evidence of his anointing. And I suspect most of us would be uncomfortable with the picture of Joel Osteen asking for donations on a remote broadcast from his yacht. Indeed, it's easy to detest name-it-and-claim-it as just sanctified greed. We are rightly suspicious that this is just the wolf of consumerism in sheep's clothing.

But how many of us are still quite comfortable with more low-grade (or soft-sell) versions of a prosperity gospel? For instance, how many of us buy into a logic that assumes that if a Christian is wealthy, they have been "blessed" by God (as if material prosperity were a kind of magic, rather than the product of often-unjust systems)? While many of us might be quick to loudly denounce the heresy of the prosperity gospel, we're quite comfortable with affirming the good of affluence. But isn't that just a prosperity gospel without the glam?

What's Right with Prosperity?

So maybe it's fair for us to ask, What's *right* with the prosperity gospel? One of the reasons why it's important to ask this question is because of the explosion of world Christianity. As you probably know, world Christianity *is* basically charismatic Christianity, and the prosperity gospel often attends pentecostal and charismatic spirituality.

But here's my question: Does the prosperity gospel mean something different in rural Nigeria than in suburban Dallas? Is the promise of material and economic abundance received differently by those who live on less than $2 a day? The prosperity gospel (for all its failures) might be an unwitting testimony to the holistic aspects of pentecostal spirituality that value the goodness of creation and embodiment—a holism that resonates with the holism of the Reformed tradition. In a curious way, the prosperity gospel is a testament to the very "worldliness" of pentecostal theology. While pentecostal spirituality might often be associated with "pie in the sky" pietism and a sort of Gnostic escapism, the prosperity gospel is one of the most un-Gnostic moments of pentecostal spirituality, refusing to spiritualize the promise that the gospel is good news for the poor. It is evidence of a core affirmation that God cares about our bellies and bodies. Granted, this means something very different in the comfort of an air-conditioned megachurch in suburban Atlanta (where "prosperity" signals an idolatrous, consumerist accumulation of luxury) as opposed to what "prosperity" promises in famished refugee camps in Rwanda. The former deserves our criticism; the latter, I think, requires careful listening.

Two Cheers for Prosperity

God's economy of abundance has no room for some romantic celebration of poverty and lack. Even if we're rightly concerned about the prosperity gospel, that shouldn't translate into any simplistic demonization of abundance or even prosperity. Indeed, this reminds me of the lyrics of an old Everclear song, "I Will Buy You a New Life":

> I hate those people who love to tell you,
> "Money is the root of all that kills."
> They have never been poor,
> They have never had the joy of a welfare Christmas.

I suggest that implicit in the prosperity gospel—and buried under all its perversions and distortions—is a lingering testament that God is concerned with the material conditions of the poor. And God's economy does not just envision some bare-minimum survival, but a flourishing, thriving abundance. The new Jerusalem is not some spartan, frugal space but rather a city teeming with downright luxury—a luxury enjoyed by all. In a similar way, the marriage supper of the Lamb doesn't have to observe the frugality of a downsized corporate lunch policy! Creation's abundance is mirrored and expanded in the new creation. Prosperity has a biblical ring to it.

However, we are still waiting for the new Jerusalem. And I think we can rightly be concerned that the prosperity gospel is often inattentive to this. Instead, the prosperity gospel seems to be a kind of realized eschatology—an overemphasis on the *already* that forgets the *not yet*. It fails to recognize that such prosperity is still *to come*. And in the meantime, it misses the structural injustices that yield abundance for only a few. In other words, the prosperity gospel fails to discern how wealth is often generated by *systems* of exploitation and oppression.

So how can we respond? On the one hand, the biblical narrative paints a picture of abundance, plenitude, and overflowing generosity as part of the warp and woof of God's creation. On the other hand, in our fallen, broken world, the prophets consistently denounce those economic systems that concentrate wealth and abundance in the hands of the few, and often at the expense of the many. So are we called to be present-day ascetics who are just waiting for an abundance to come? Doesn't that seem like we'd be spurning the gifts of God's creational abundance?

Fasting and Feasting

The answer, I suggest, revolves around how we inhabit *time*. An intentional asceticism or abstinence that voluntarily chooses to forgo abundance attests to the persistent injustice of current economic systems, expressing solidarity with the poor and refusing the idolatry of materialism. But such can run the risk of spurning God's abundance and can unwittingly fall prey to a logic of scarcity. On the other hand, an unmitigated enjoyment of abundance in the present almost inevitably lives off the exploitation of others and is prone to idolatry.[2] So it seems we're faced with two problematic options.

But it's not either-or if we think about this dynamically with respect to *time*—which is exactly the idea behind ancient and medieval practices of fasting and feasting. The rhythm of fasting and feasting calls the people of God to bear witness to both of these realities at different times and in different seasons: we rightly celebrate and enjoy God's abundance, but we also rightly lament and resist injustice and poverty. During days or seasons of fasting—which, in a way, should be the default habit of the church's sojourn—we say no to abundance as a witness to the fact that so many lack not only abundance but what's needed just to survive. But during days and seasons of feasting, we enjoy a foretaste of the abundance of the coming kingdom.

The God who became poor so that we might become rich invites us into a way of life marked by the rhythms of fasting and feasting—as a way of making us hungry for the abundant life.

Notes

1. Walter Brueggemann, "The Liturgy of Abundance, the Myth of Scarcity," *Christian Century* (March 24–31, 1999): 342.

2. Recall Paul's connection of the two: "Put to death, therefore, whatever belongs to your earthly nature: sexual immorality, impurity, lust, evil desires and *greed*, which is *idolatry*" (Col. 3:5).

17

A LETTER TO YOUNG PARENTS

Dear Grace and Alex,

Congratulations! Thanks be to God for the safe arrival of what sounds like a packed little bundle of hope: my goodness, 10 lbs., 6 oz.! It must be the milk there in Wisconsin.

Well, on behalf of the rest of us exhausted, grateful, and terrified inhabitants, let me welcome you to a strange new world: parenthood. This is going to be the hardest thing you've ever done, and it's worth every bit of the blood, sweat, and tears that are to come. You can't imagine that now. I understand. Soak up every ounce of joy and elation and starry-eyed wonder at the miracle of baby Liam. I'll be watching as the terror sets in. It's usually when you're headed out the hospital door that it hits you: "They're actually letting me take this little creature home? But I don't know what the hell I'm doing!" Yeah, get used to that.

But also remember this: in a few weeks, you're going to

This letter first appeared in a special issue of *Comment* magazine that I guest-edited as a collection of "Letters to the Young," *Comment* (Spring 2011): 20–21. Reprinted with permission.

bring Liam forward for baptism. In that sacramental act he is going to be tangibly marked with the sign of God's promises. That should be a first reminder that you're not in this alone—that Liam is being claimed by a promise-keeping Father who is even more faithful than you. There will be days and seasons when that will be an unspeakable comfort to you.

In the sacrament of baptism, not only will you claim God's promises, you'll be confessing that you alone are not able to raise Liam. The baptismal ceremony is, I think, a wonderful gift to parents who rightly approach their task with fear and trembling. For while you, in response to God's promise, will make promises to God about how you will raise Liam, the congregation will also make a promise—to come alongside you, to support you and nourish you, to sustain you all within the household of God that is bigger than the three of you. So baptism is a sign that our homes are open, interdependent households, not closed, nuclear units. Baptism signals that all of us—married or single, parent or child—are part of a larger household that is the church of God, and together, that household has pledged to be one big community of godparents. When you run up against the challenges of parenting, don't be scared to remind the church of the promise it made to you.

I hope and pray that your labor as parents can be buoyed by these promises and this sense that your tiny, growing family will flourish just to the extent that you center yourselves in the "first family," which is the church. You will need this, believe me. One of the terrible lies of our culture—and even the rhetoric of "family values"—is the crippling myth that our homes are self-sufficient incubators for child rearing. If you buy into that myth, you'll isolated by a constant sense of failure. For it won't take long to realize that you are not able to do this on your own, even though you're an intertwined team. But if you've bought into the myth of the self-sufficient family, you also won't be willing to admit that you need help. Baptism is the church's way of signaling right from the get-go that we know you need help! We know you can't do this on your own. So we're not going to be surprised or disappointed or judgmental when you lean on us. We'll be there waiting. Why not get into the habit early?

Finally, while I don't mean to rain on the parade of your joy, I do feel compelled to share the bad news, too: Liam might break your heart. Actually, Liam *is* going to break your heart. Somehow. Somewhere. Maybe more than once. To become a parent is to promise you'll love prodigals. Indeed, some days parenting is exactly how God is going to teach you to love your enemies. Because there'll be days when a 17-year-old Liam is going to see *you* as the enemy, and all of a sudden you'll realize that the Sermon on the Mount is not about war and foreign policy, nor is it just "pie in the sky" piety: instead, you'll hear those words anew and realize that in the command to love your enemies, Jesus is calling you to follow him *as* a parent, and sometimes even that task will look cruciform. It will require absorbing all Liam's misplaced animosity, all his confused attempts to figure out who (and whose) he is. At those moments, Jesus's call to lay down your life and take up the cross will have a mundane tangibility you could have never imagined. Some days, loving Liam is going to require you to turn the other cheek and absorb that heartbreak like a slap across the face. And it's then that you'll most want to remember the promises of a faithful Father that trickled down his little forehead years ago.

But those painful moments will be overshadowed by a million others. You're going to think it's incredible when Liam smiles, or says "Mama," or rolls over on his tummy, but let me tell you: that won't even compare to the afternoon when, in what feels like an out-of-body experience, you realize you're having a conversation with this *man*—you might be sitting on the front porch talking about Mumford & Sons or Andy Warhol or World War II artillery, and for a moment you can hardly believe that the little bundle you brought home from the hospital has grown into this beautiful, mystifying, wonderful young man. And you realize that, in your son, God has given you one of your best friends in the whole world, and you try to suppress your smile while thinking to yourself, "Thank you, thank you, thank you, thank you."

It's all worth it,
Jamie

18

An Open Letter
to Praise Bands

Dear Praise Band,

I so appreciate your willingness and desire to offer up your gifts to God in worship. I appreciate your devotion and celebrate your faithfulness—schlepping to church early, Sunday after Sunday; making time for practice mid-week; learning and writing new songs; and so much more. Like those skilled artists and artisans whom God used to create the tabernacle (Exod. 36), you are willing to put your artistic gifts in service to the triune God.

So please receive this little missive in the spirit it is meant: as an encouragement to reflect on the *practice* of "leading worship." It seems to me that you are often simply co-opted into a practice without being encouraged to reflect on its rationale, its reason why. In other words, it seems to me that you are often recruited to "lead worship" without much opportunity to pause and reflect on the nature of "worship" and what it would mean to "lead."

In particular, my concern is that we, the church, have

unwittingly encouraged you to simply import musical practices *into* Christian worship that—while they might be appropriate elsewhere—are detrimental to congregational worship. More pointedly, using language I first employed in *Desiring the Kingdom*, I sometimes worry that we've unwittingly encouraged you to import certain *forms of performance* that are, in effect, secular liturgies and not just neutral methods. Without us realizing it, the dominant practices of performance train us to relate to music (and musicians) in a certain way: as something for our pleasure, as entertainment, as a largely passive experience. The function and goal of music in these secular liturgies is quite different from the function and goal of music in Christian worship.

So let me offer just a few brief axioms with the hope of encouraging new reflection on the practice of "leading worship":

1. If we, the congregation, can't hear ourselves, it's not worship. Christian worship is not a concert. In a concert (a particular form of performance), we often expect to be overwhelmed by sound, particularly in certain styles of music. In a concert, we come to expect that weird sort of sensory deprivation that happens from sensory overload, when the pounding of the bass on our chest and the wash of music over the crowd leaves us with the rush of a certain aural vertigo. And there's nothing wrong with concerts! It's just that Christian worship is not a concert. Christian worship is a collective, communal, congregational practice—and the gathered sound and harmony of a congregation singing *as one* is integral to the practice of worship. It is a way of performing the reality that, in Christ, we are one body. But that requires that we actually be able to hear ourselves and hear our sisters and brothers singing alongside us. When the amped sound of the praise band overwhelms congregational voices, we can't hear ourselves sing, so we lose that communal aspect of the congregation and are encouraged to effectively become private, passive worshipers.

2. If we, the congregation, can't sing along, it's not worship. In other forms of musical performance, musicians and bands will want to improvise and be creative, offering new renditions and exhibiting their virtuosity with all sorts of different trills and pauses and improvisations on the received tune. Again, that can be a delightful aspect of a concert, but in Christian worship it just means that we, the congregation, can't sing along. And so your virtuosity gives rise to our passivity; your creativity simply encourages our silence. And while *you* may be worshiping *through* your creativity, the same creativity actually shuts down congregational song.

3. If *you*, the praise band, are the center of attention, it's not worship. I know it's generally not your fault that we've put you at the front of the church. And I know you want to *model* worship for us to imitate. But because we've encouraged you to basically import forms of performance from the concert venue into the sanctuary, we might not realize that we've also unwittingly encouraged a sense that you are the center of attention. And when your performance becomes a display of your virtuosity—even with the best of intentions—it's difficult to counter the temptation to make the praise band the focus of our attention. When the praise band goes into long riffs that you might intend as offerings to God, we the congregation become utterly passive, and because we've adopted habits of relating to music from the Grammys and the concert venue, we unwittingly make you the center of attention. I wonder if there might be some intentional reflection on *placement* (to the side? leading from behind?) and performance that might help us counter these habits we bring with us to worship.

Please consider these points carefully and recognize what I am *not* saying. This isn't just some plea for traditional worship and a critique of contemporary worship. Don't mistake this as a defense of pipe organs and a critique of guitars and drums (or banjos and mandolins). My concern isn't with *style*, but with *form*: What are we trying to do when we lead worship? If we are intentional about worship as a communal, congregational practice that brings us into a dialogical encounter with the living God—about it being not merely expressive but also formative—then we can do that with cellos or steel guitars, pipe organs or African drums.

Much, much more could be said. But let me stop here, and please receive this as the encouragement it's meant to be. I would love to see you continue to offer your artistic gifts in worship to the triune God who is teaching us a new song.

Most sincerely,
Jamie

19

THE OTHER SIDE OF ATHENS

Theology, Culture, and Sports

The perennial question concerning the relationship between Athens and Jerusalem was foreshadowed in Saint Paul's own encounter in the city: as indicated by his visit to Mars Hill, Athens represented to Paul a capital of ideas and a hub of philosophical thought. But he also recognized that in, behind, and under philosophy was, in fact, a whole cadre of *religious* impulses—religious impulses that, in the context of Athens, gave rise to a plethora of idolatries. And yet even this idolatry was a witness to something about the nature of human persons as created: we are religious animals, and even when that structural desire for transcendence is warped and misdirected, the very misdirections (idolatries) continue to bear witness to a creational stamp upon our nature.

Paul's engagement with the philosophers at Mars Hill,

This essay was written as a foreword to *The Image of God in the Human Body: Essays on Christianity and Sports*, ed. Donald Lee Deardorff and John White (Lewiston, NY: Edwin Mellen Press, 2008). Reprinted with permission.

and Tertullian's later posing of the question about the relationship between "Athens" and "Jerusalem," have generated a long tradition of Christian reflection on culture—the habits, practices, and institutions of human making (*poiēsis*) that unfold the potential of creation. Thus the poles of "Jerusalem" and "Athens" would later be transposed as "Christ" and "culture"[1] or "church" and "world." Of course, there has been a long tradition—let's call it pietistic—that has largely written off the latter pole as sinful. In such cases, "culture" is synonymous with "the world" of 1 John 2:15–17 or James 4:4. But the authors of this volume, working from a sensibility that I would describe as Augustinian and Reformed, eschew such pietism and begin instead from an affirmation of the goodness of creation—and hence an affirmation of the creational task of human culture-making. Being image bearers of God means being culture makers called to unfold the potential that has been folded into creation. Eden wasn't created with bookstores, concert halls, and universities. These cultural institutions—and many more!—are the fruit of creatures taking up the tasks given to them by the Creator, channeling their gifts and talents to encourage the flourishing of all creation—what the Bible calls *shalom*. The fall and brokenness of creation means that we often do this badly: our cultural unfoldings can and often do go against the grain of the universe. But this does not mean that culture per se is an evil. The problem is *how*, not *what*: at issue is *how* we "cultivate" creation. In fact, it's not even a question of *whether*: as creatures we have a cultural impulsion that can't be turned off. It might be distorted and misdirected, but it can't be shut down. This is why, when Paul strolled the idolatrous agora of Athens, he could nonetheless find in the idolatry a witness and testimony to something about human nature as created by God.[2]

So an essential feature of the goodness of creation is that humans are created as *cultural* animals. And it is this creational impulse that has generated the rich fabric of civilization that we enjoy, from papyri to iPods. Theological reflection on culture began by taking "Athens" as a sort of placeholder or crystallization of cultural energies: Athens represented the culture of theory and philosophy, what we might today associate with the university. Thus considering the question of "Athens and Jerusalem" was a way of thinking about the relationship of the gospel to other ideas and worldviews—these being a key aspect of human culture. Over time the conversation partners expanded: Christians also began thinking about the relationship between Jerusalem and Rome (politics), Jerusalem and Vienna (music), Jerusalem and Hollywood (film), Jerusalem and Manchester (industry, technology) or Jerusalem and Tokyo (the market, economics), and so on. But as the authors of this volume rightly note—and seek to correct—it is stunning that, despite rich reflections on aspects of culture such as the arts, commerce, healthcare, education, and technology, to this point the Christian tradition has largely failed to articulate a robust reflection on the *other* side of Athens, its Olympian side—the Athens of sports and games. This lacuna in Christian theological reflection on culture is puzzling given both the ancient and persistent tradition of athletics and its contemporary dominance in our culture—having become a multibillion dollar worldwide industry and a way of life that inspires a not-so-metaphorical "religious" devotion for many. And yet one will be hard-pressed to find Christian theological reflection on sports as a cultural phenomenon. When one pauses to consider the centrality of sports in our globalized culture (one could simply add up the hours of television air time devoted to sports in a given week), it is truly remarkable that there are not shelves upon shelves of such work. But not even the recent explosion of theological reflection on popular culture seems to be attentive to sports. Indeed, where is Manchester United, the New York Yankees, and ESPN in the plethora of material on "theology and popular culture?"[3]

So where can we find sustained theological reflection on sports? I don't mean "religious" reflections by athletes—which are usually testimonials that simply instrumentalize sports as a means for sharing a message about a wholly other-worldly, disembodied "gospel" (and which tend to also be remarkably unreflective and uncritical about the nature of sports as industry in our culture). The authors in this book are at the vanguard of much-needed reflection on this central aspect of contemporary culture—and this aspect of the creational mandate. For as they suggest in various places, many features of sports and athletics can be affirmed as good, creational unfoldings of potential that God folded into creation—unpacking potential in our bodies and our relationships. *Play* is an essential aspect of creational, communal life. One might say that there were games in Eden, and because we confess the resurrection of the body, we hold out hope that there will be games in the new Jerusalem. In between, there are some hard questions that demand serious theological reflection. While we can appreciate *play* as a feature of creation, is *competition*? Or how are we to think about sports in an era of its commodification and commercialization—when the other side of Athens is so closely wed to Wall Street? And what about when sports *becomes* religion? How can we think critically about the idolatry of sports without lapsing into a reactionary pietism?[4]

These are only a small taste of the range of questions that need to be asked about this central cultural phenomenon. Surprisingly, up to this point, Christians and Christian theologians have not been asking them; thus we lack a robust theology of sports. This book makes a bold move to change that. The authors in this book ably step into a massive lacuna and seek to launch a discussion and field. Granted, being on the vanguard is risky business: there are so many questions to be asked that sometimes the best thing we can do is to first just try to get all the questions on the table. But this book not only articulates the questions, it also begins, with wisdom, to articulate some answers. Above all, it serves the community of both theologians and athletes by playfully inviting us to consider what it means for those of us on Jerusalem's team to visit the other side of Athens.

Notes

1. I think, however, that there are good reasons to bid farewell to this Niebuhrian taxonomy, in particular because it seems to "pristinate" what is really much messier and more complicated. For instance, it seems to suggest that "culture" is not religious and that religion ("Christ") is not cultural—both of which are false. The result is a false dichotomy. For further articulation of the problem with Niebuhr's framework, see Craig A. Carter, *Rethinking Christ and Culture: A Post-Christendom Perspective* (Grand Rapids, MI: Brazos Press, 2006). Nonetheless, the Christ/culture taxonomy is so pervasive that, especially for an

emergent field such as theology and sports, it is understandable that one might first work within the existing paradigm.

2. Cf. Augustine's account of how Rome's penchant for a bastardized peace was nonetheless a sign of a structural feature of human communities (*City of God*, XIX) or John Calvin's similar argument regarding idolatry as a persistent witness to the *sensus divinitatis* implanted within humanity (*Institutes*, I.iii).

3. Given the overwhelming commercial and cultural influence of sports, it is surprising that it receives such slim treatment in recent works such as Kelton Cobb's *Blackwell Guide to Theology and Popular Culture* (Oxford: Blackwell, 2005); Gordon Lynch's *Understanding Theology and Popular Culture* (Oxford: Blackwell, 2004); and, most recently, *Everyday Theology: How to Read Cultural Texts and Interpret Trends*, ed. K. Vanhoozer, C. A. Anderson, and M. J. Sleasman (Grand Rapids, MI: Baker Academic, 2007). While these works allude to the significance of sports, the present book seeks to expand and deepen this concern. [Since the original publication of this essay, an important book on just this topic has appeared: Shirl James Hoffman, *Good Game: Christianity and the Culture of Sports* (Waco, TX: Baylor University Press, 2010).]

4. One finds a surprising source for considering the idolatry of sports in Tom Wolfe's recent novel, *I Am Charlotte Simmons* (New York: Farrar, Strauss and Giroux, 2004).

20

Can Hope Be Wrong?

On the New Universalism

This ain't your grandma's universalism (if your grandma was, say, a Unitarian). The (relatively) old universalism was a liberal universalism of "many roads to God, who is a big cuddly grandpa" (or, more recently, grand*ma*). Such a universalism was generally embarrassed by Christian particularity and any claims to the divinity of Christ. Instead, Jesus was a kindly teacher like so many others pointing us all to that great kumbaya sing-along in the beyond.

In contrast, the new universalism is an evangelical universalism, a christocentric universalism. If all will be saved, they will be saved *in Christ*, because of the work of Christ as the Incarnate God who has triumphed over the power of sin and death (the new universalist Christ is a victor more than a redeemer).

This essay (and its appendix), which originally appeared on my blog, *Fors Clavigera*, arose from some conversations spawned by the publication of Rob Bell's controversial book, *Love Wins* (San Francisco: HarperOne, 2011)—though this is not a review of that book.

The question, then, is, just what *compels* one to be an evangelical universalist? Some resort to prooftexting, operating with a naïve, selective reading of Scripture. I'm going to do the evangelical universalist a favor and ignore such a strategy, only because I think it can be so easily refuted. (Many of these evangelical universalists would critically pounce on such selective prooftexting in other contexts.)

No, the motivation for evangelical universalism is not really a close reading of the Bible's claims about eternity. Instead, it seems that the macromotivation for evangelical universalism is less a text and more a hermeneutic, a kind of sensibility about the very nature of God as love (which includes its own implicit assumptions about the nature of love). Two phrases you will often hear from evangelical universalists involve *hope* and our *imagination*. (For a sample combination of this constellation of concerns, see Lauren Winner's essay on Rob Bell in the *New York Times Book Review* [April 22, 2011].) The concern is often formulated in the following ways, and often in tandem:

1. **"I can't imagine"** that a God of love would condemn Gandhi to hell. (Always Gandhi. Why Gandhi? As Ross Douthat asked in a *New York Times* column: Can you insert Tony Soprano here? Doesn't the evangelical universalist case of Gandhi imply a kind of salvation by works? But I digress . . .) Or, as Winner puts it, evangelical universalists "can't imagine their secular friends aren't going to heaven."

2. "I don't *know* if all will be saved but **I hope** this will be true." I'm firmly committed to the particularity of Christ, the evangelical universalist will emphasize. I just *hope* that

God's salvation is not so particular that he only saves some. And it is precisely God's love and mercy that make me hope in this way.

The question, then, is this: Are these hopes and imaginings sufficiently *warranted* to overturn the received, orthodox doctrines concerning final judgment and eternal damnation? Are these sufficient to overturn the narrative thrust of Scripture and the clearer reading of biblical passages that suggest otherwise. (Let's stop making this just about passages that mention hell; at issue here are all passages that discuss *judgment*.) Are these hopes and imaginings sufficient for me to set aside centuries of the church's theological reflection on these matters? Is my chronological snobbery warranted? Just how do I think *my* hopes and imaginings are somehow more faithful and merciful and just than the generations upon generations of my forebears' in the Christian faith? (I'll confess to being a kind of theological Burkean: it's very hard for me to imagine that I am smarter or better than Augustine or John Calvin or Jonathan Edwards. I'm not generally given to whiggish theology.)

Let's attend to these two specific sorts of claims. I would note that both of these intuitions are fundamentally anthropocentric strategies, outcomes of what Charles Taylor (in *A Secular Age*) calls "the anthropocentric turn" in modernity. A couple of thoughts:

1. The "I can't imagine" strategy is fundamentally Feuerbachian: it is a hermeneutic of *projection* that begins from what *I* can conceive and then projects upward, as it were, to

a conception of God. While this "imagining" might have absorbed some biblical themes of love and mercy, the absorption seems selective. More importantly, the "I can't imagine" argument seems inattentive to how much my imagination is shaped and limited by all kinds of cultural factors and sensibilities—including how I imagine the nature of love, etc. The "I can't imagine" argument makes man the measure of God, or at least seems to let the limits and constraints of *my* imagination trump the authority of Scripture and interpretation. I take it that discipleship means submitting even my imagination to the discipline of Scripture. (Indeed, could anything be more countercultural right now than Jonathan Edwards's radical *theocentrism*, with all its attendant scandals for our modern sensibilities?)

2. The "at least I hope" strategy might seem less problematic. Doesn't it just name what all of us secretly desire? Indeed, wouldn't we be quite inhuman if we *didn't* hope in this way? (Then you get Winner's obnoxious suggestion that any of those who continue to affirm divine judgment are really trying to "guard heaven's gate," taking a certain delight in exclusion, as if they saw heaven as a country club. I won't dignify that with a response.)

But whence this hope? Can our hopes ever be *wrong*? Let's try an analogous example: I love my wife dearly. She is the best thing that ever happened to me, and our marriage has been an incredible means of grace in my life. I can't imagine life without her; indeed, I don't want to imagine life without her. And I want to hope that we will share this intimacy as a husband and wife *forever*.

But then I run into this claim from Jesus: "At the resurrection people will neither marry nor be given in marriage; they will be like the angels in heaven" (Matt. 22:30). Should I nonetheless *hope* that marriage endures in eternity? Should I profess that I can't *know* this (since Scripture seems to suggest otherwise), but nonetheless claim that somehow *hoping* it might be true is still faithful? Or should I submit even my hopes to discipline by the authority of Scripture?

The new universalism is not the old universalism. Fair enough. But those of us who reject even the new universalism aren't gleeful about it. We might even *wish* it were otherwise. But we also recognize that even our wishes, hopes, and desires need discipline.

Appendix: A Response to Critics
[The following was part of a postscript to my original essay, written in response to various sorts of criticisms that arose in the blogosphere. I have only reproduced those parts of the postscript which I think I have some enduring value.]

I'm afraid none of the responses have really given me pause about my concerns. And I'm not going to engage in some point-by-point refutation. If you think that means I don't have an argument or a defense, go crazy: you're welcome to do that. However, let me make just a couple of clarifications:

1. I still think the "motivation" question is a legitimate one (though obviously not the only one—do I seriously have to state that? Apparently.). In this regard, I just take myself to be following some of Charles Taylor's methodology in *A*

Secular Age. Indeed, for those who really care about this issue, I think *A Secular Age* (pp. 650ff.) is important reading: there Taylor examines the shift in plausibility conditions that engendered the "decline in Hell." I take my point to be a sort of off-handed cousin of his analysis.

The question would just be something like this: if there is such a "clear," "biblical" logic that impels us toward universalism, why did the majority of Christendom seem to miss this for 1500–1800 years? There are multiple accounts of that. Taylor's account is one of *motivations*: as he argues, something changes in "modern Christian consciousness" that makes us *want* something else to be the case, thus priming us to see it there all along. That might not be an adequate account, but it is certainly a legitimate aspect of an account. And if you don't think this is really what's at work for all sorts of folks who don't read theology, well . . . then you haven't read Lauren Winner's essay.

But actually the better parallel from Taylor is found elsewhere in *A Secular Age*, where Taylor considers conversions to unbelief (pp. 362–66). This section of Taylor's book is a fascinating little psychoanalysis of a convert—but of one (or a culture) that has converted from belief to unbelief. The upshot is a hermeneutics of suspicion: if someone tells you that they've converted to unbelief because of science, don't believe them. Because what's usually captivated them is not scientific evidence per se, but the *form* of science: "Even where the conclusions of science seem to be doing the work of conversion, it is very often not the detailed findings so much as the form" (p. 362). Indeed, "the appeal of scientific materialism is not so much the cogency of its detailed findings as that of the underlying epistemological stance, and that for ethical reasons. It is seen as the stance of maturity, of courage, of manliness, over against childish fears and sentimentality" (p. 365). But you can also understand how, on the retelling, the convert to unbelief will want to give the impression that it was the scientific evidence that was doing the work (p. 365). Converts to unbelief always tell subtraction stories.

And the belief that they've converted *from* has usually been an immature, Sunday-Schoolish faith that could be easily toppled. So while such converts to unbelief tell themselves stories about growing up and facing reality—and thus paint belief as essentially immature and childish—what they betray is the simplistic shape of the faith they've abandoned. "If our faith has remained at the stage of the immature images, then the story that materialism equals maturity can seem plausible" (p. 365). But in fact their conversion to unbelief was also a conversion to a new faith: "faith in science's ability" (p. 366). The point is that people convert to positions *not* on the basis of reasons but on the basis of certain moral stances associated with the positions. It seems to me there's something similar at work in what I'd call zeitgeist-universalism.

2. What I was probably also reacting to in my original blog post was the general tenor of moral superiority that so often (not always) accompanies evangelical universalists. I'm really tired of all the construals of universalism that basically make it seem that only moral monsters could *not* be universalists. So was Augustine stupid? Or malicious? Or both?

3. Finally, with respect to my basic claim that hope can be

wrong: surely no one would suggest that hope gets some kind of free pass—as if a hope couldn't be "wrong" in the sense of being mis-directed or mis-ordered. So I take it that, in principle, as a virtue, hope is subject to discipline, one might say. Hope doesn't traffic in some neutral domain where you can hope whatever you want. Therefore, in principle, hopes could be subject to chastisement (isn't this half the critique of the prosperity gospel?).

So I take it to be formally true that a hope can be wrong. Then we'd have to discuss *on what grounds* a hope for universalism could be right or wrong. Just because it's a "nice" hope doesn't give it a free pass; just because it *seems* to be a "logical" hope doesn't suffice. Indeed, I think Jonathan Edwards would argue that what *I* hope for is quite beside the point; in other words, there might be a more theocentric way to frame this whole conversation.

21

(LIBERAL) SKEPTICISM
VS. (ORTHODOX) DOUBT

There are certain streams of "emerging" Christianity that seem to think doubt is some revolutionary new stance that finally has permission to emerge now that we are "new kinds of Christians." Formerly oppressed by fundamentalisms that quashed any hint of uncertainty, such Christians are at pains to point out that we can never be certain. But having still accepted the modern equation of knowledge with certainty, they also end up professing that we can't *know*. So what we're left with is not doubt, but skepticism.

It seems that those who think permission to doubt is some radically new possibility for Christians are the same people who think that a concern for justice is some secret message of Jesus heretofore hidden from Christianity, when in fact it just means that it was hidden *from them* in the pietistic enclaves of their early formation. In a similar way, doubt is as old as faith. As Kierkegaard suggested in one of his journals, "Doubt comes into the world through faith." As I've suggested elsewhere (in a chapter on doubt in *The Devil Reads Derrida*), some of our greatest saints have been our greatest doubters, too. Some of our exemplary believers have also been masters of suspicion. The new kind of doubters have nothing on the likes of Graham Greene or Mother Teresa or Bernanos's country priest or Endo's Jesuit missionaries.

But there is also an important difference between emergent skeptics and catholic doubters: The new kind of skeptics want the faith to be cut down to the size of their doubt, to conform to their suspicions. Doubt is taken to be sufficient warrant for jettisoning what occasions our disbelief and discomfort, cutting a scandalizing God down to the size of our believing. For the new doubters, if I can't believe it, it can't be true. If orthodoxy is unbelievable, then let's come up with a rendition we *can* believe in.

But for catholic doubters, God is not subject to my doubts. Rather, like the movements of a lament psalm, all of the scandalizing, unbelievable aspects of an inscrutable God are the *target* of my doubts—but the catholic doubter would never dream that this is an occasion for revising the faith, cutting it down to the measure of what I can live with. It's not a matter of coming up with a gospel I can live with; it's a matter of learning to live with all of the scandal of the gospel, and that can take a lifetime. Graham Greene's "whiskey priest" doesn't for a moment think that the church should revise its doctrine and standards in order to make him feel comfortable about his fornication—even if he might lament what seems to be a denial of some feature of his humannness. All of his doubts and suspicion and resistance are not skeptical gambits that set him off in search of a liberal Christianity he can live with; they are, instead, features of a life of sanctification, or lack thereof. And no one is surprised by that. The prayer of the doubter is not "Lord I believe, conform to the measure of my unbelief," but rather "Lord I believe, *help* thou my unbelief."

For just this reason orthodox, catholic faith has always been able to absorb doubt as a feature of discipleship: indeed, the church is full of doubters. It is the grace of our scandalous God that welcomes them.

22

THE SECULARIZATION OF THANKSGIVING AND THE SACRALIZATION OF THE MILITARY

I have a deep ambivalence about Thanksgiving as a holiday. For example, it's not properly part of the (transnational) church's liturgical year, and it tends to be easily conflated with American civil religion and to paper over the history of colonialism. But while the "official" holiday is at least questionable, certainly gratitude and thanksgiving are central to the Christian life. Indeed, in the organization of the Heidelberg Catechism, the entirety of the Christian life is encompassed under the rubric of *gratitude*.

So, ambivalence aside, it doesn't take much coaxing for me to take a day to enjoy a feast and football with family and friends (even if that means having to watch the Detroit Lions and the Dallas Cowboys). But my friend Mark and I both commented again this year on how puzzling it was to see the incessant military references and images on the Thanksgiving broadcasts. It was like the NFL was somehow broadcasting on Memorial Day or the Fourth of July. Why would Thanksgiving be so interconnected with the armed forces?

But I think I've discerned the logic to this and crystallized the linkage. For some reason, broadcast television always feels compelled to secularize religious and quasi-religious holidays; this is, in some ways, part and parcel of other secularizing currents in commercial culture. But when Thanksgiving is secularized, what's lost is precisely the Object to whom we would render gratitude. In other words, we end up being thankful for gifts without being able to recognize the Giver.

So we come up with a substitute Giver, which is something like the *idea* of "America"—the land of the free. And while there are alternative conceptual histories that would actually honor how much the United States was *conceptually* forged—that the US is really the experimental product of *ideas*—our current anti-intellectual climate would rather think of "America" as the product of force and might (as the national anthem prefers). So if we are thankful *for* America, we're thankful *to* the military who, proverbially, protect our freedom, keep us free, make the ultimate sacrifice for our freedom, etc. Soldiers are thus revered as the warrior-priests of freedom.

And what are we free *for*? Well, *to shop*. And so the best expression of thanksgiving is precisely Black Friday, that Dionysian display of consumerist passion when people literally die in the frantic pursuit of consumer goods. In sum, the secularization of thanksgiving leads to the sacralization of the military as the guardians of consumer freedom.

Such secularization, then, is not a-religious but *otherwise-religious*. Thus a secularized thanksgiving yields a uniquely American idolatry.

23

Desiring the Kingdom in a Postmodern World

An Interview

Caleb Maskell: *Desiring the Kingdom* is a book that I've been recommending strongly to folks in the Vineyard, because it gets at the heart of some of the issues of self-understanding that I think we are currently facing as a community of churches. Some Christians have understood themselves to be defined chiefly by statements of belief: what we think about God most defines who we are. Other Christians have understood themselves more in terms of action: the things we do and our ways of being in the world most define who are. You take up this debate in *Desiring the Kingdom*, suggesting that we are actually described by what we love. Could you talk about that a bit?

This interview first appeared in *Cutting Edge* (Fall 2011): 12–18, the church planting magazine of the Association of Vineyard Churches. This grew out of my plenary address to the Society for Vineyard Scholars the year before, at the instigation of Caleb Maskell. Reprinted with permission.

James K. A. Smith: I think it's important to recognize that the picture of us as thinking things—or the picture that defined us by what we believed in terms of propositional assents to doctrines—is, in itself, a fairly recently acquired habit.

That shift in the picture of humanity which emphasized the talking-head, top-heavy, idea-centric, intellectualist model of the human person is a bit of an acquired taste, which we acquired from modernism and shifts that took place in modernism. As it turns out, that's just a bad picture of human beings. It's not a good functional appreciation for the complexity of who we are as humans.

That's why I think postmodernism and postmodernity are an occasion for the church—especially Protestant and evangelical churches—to wake up to the fact of how much we bought into that modern picture of the human subject. In doing so, we forgot something of the biblical and historical Christian wisdom that gave us a richer, more holistic account of who we are. What defines me is not primarily what I think, or even what I believe in terms of the propositions to which I give assent. What defines me is what I love, what I long for, what I desire. It's located in the affective core of my person.

To get that point is not a matter of "getting with it" in a postmodern culture. It's not, "Oh, well, this is the new way of thinking about being human." It's actually just that a postmodern critique of modernism has been an opportunity for the church to remember what we used to know. We can go back to appreciating a more holistic and affective picture of the human person.

CM: So this idea—that we're chiefly defined as human beings by an account of the things that we love—is an older idea than the idea that we're defined by our beliefs, not some newfangled postmodern innovation?

JKAS: Right. But nothing is wrong with believing. Believing is good. It's just that believing is actually the articulation of what we love. It is a kind of understanding we have of God that can't always be fully articulated. That's why you can articulate what Christians believe, and it's not wrong. But this sense that what really defines us is what we love; what we long for; what we desire—that picture of the human being as lover is an ancient picture. I think Saint Augustine is one of the people who articulates so powerfully that we are made for love. The question isn't whether you love; it's what you love. That has all kinds of implications for how you go about evangelism.

But I also think it's a deeply biblical idea. In Colossians 3, when Paul writes to the Colossian Christians and exhorts them to put on Christ, it is putting on love. Paul says, "Clothe yourselves in compassion." Immediately after that, he starts talking about the practices of worship: singing psalms and hymns and spiritual songs, being devoted to the Word and engaging in prayer.

So there's a connection there that I think the Scriptures convey. It gives us a much more holistic picture of who we are as persons.

CM: I think there's a sense in which the picture of a human being as lover resonates deeply with some of the intuitive practices that we have in the Vineyard. For example, we've always prioritized worship—particularly worship songs directed toward God that express love to him, for who God is and what Jesus has done.

It's the idea that love draws us forward, but we're also met with love. It's the connection of our love with God's love in terms of being pulled toward the future that's not here yet but is coming.

JKAS: Absolutely. I see this intuition that we are lovers implicitly operative in Vineyard appreciation for the affections. People can sometimes criticize what looks like a kind of romanticism of worship. But to me, it's a signal that the Vineyard recognizes that God is the Great Seducer.

God is not pushing us; God is pulling us. God is drawing us. God is attracting us. I see Vineyard worship honoring the dynamics of that lure, that draw, that wooing, in some sense.

CM: On that point, I have seen something interesting emerging lately. I think a lot of worship leaders in the Vineyard and similar movements who have valued that "affectional" aspect of worship have been struggling in some ways with the converse, which is that worship songs also put words in people's mouths about what we believe about God. The expression of affections needs to be very well articulated—because it essentially distills what we believe!

So I love the idea that beliefs are shorthand forms of practices. The songs we sing and things we do in our churches are intended to give a microcosm of what the larger picture is supposed to look like.

JKAS: Yes, and I also think you want room for a sort of feedback loop. When we go through the exercise of articulating our beliefs, that articulation can also be the basis for a critique of our practices.

So we need to keep our practices in account. For example, our worship shouldn't slide off into emotivism or the "Jesus is my boyfriend" kind of thing. Critical reflection and articulation can serve the practices.

CM: Responding to that desire for critical reflection, some Vineyard people attend Vineyard Leadership Institute, some people end up going to seminary, and some fools like myself even get PhDs. How should the training in critical reflection that people gain in these venues help to build the "feedback loop" that you're talking about in the context of the church?

JKAS: For those of us who then feel this impulsion and engage in intellectual reflection for the sake of the church, the ultimate goal and *telos* of our reflection is to have faithful practice. But if the price of admission to critical analysis is to buy into paradigms of reflection that are simply not hospitable to our communities of practice, we must have the courage to push back.

If we're asking how this kind of reflection can serve the church and happen in the church, we have to have congregations and a fellowship that have enough courage and trust to receive this reflection as a gift. The reflection will help us to be better practitioners; it will help us ultimately to be better disciples and followers of Jesus. That also requires that those of us engaged in this kind of reflection will need to take a diaconal stance. We must come in as servants, not experts.

We should ask, "How can I, with my gifts and expertise and training, help us to think anew about our practices?"

To me, that's what the church has historically called "reform." The condition of reform and renewal has always required us to find just a little bit of sympathetic distance from our practices so we can evaluate them in light of Scripture and in light of kingdom goals. It's a two-way street. As long as everyone sees that kind of reflection is good for the community, we'll create space for it.

CM: That's clearly a place where movements over the course of the history of the church have had to grow, right? It's not always clear that someone with an intellectual voice of suggestion or critique is intending to be helpful!

JKAS: Right. And sometimes they're not helpful! Sometimes there's just a snobbishness that comes when people get inculcated by academic and scholarly communities.

The other dynamic is that sometimes, in the most vibrant movements where the Spirit is afoot, you can understand why their participants are given to a certain pragmatism. They're just trying to get things done. There's work to do; the harvest is ripe.

I have a Pentecostal background. In the 20th century you can see that parallel in Pentecostalism. It was highly pragmatic. Not until later did we actually begin to see the virtue of reflection. But the virtue of reflection is that it is for the practice. It digs deep wells that you can drink from for a long, long time.

So when I'm teaching students at a seminary, if I'm trying to convince students why they need to know Hebrew, there doesn't seem to be any immediate payoff. But they must imagine that by learning Hebrew they are drilling this deep well that will withstand the drought that will come ten years into ministry. Somehow, learning Hebrew will have pastoral implications for them to carry out. This isn't just an academic hoop I make them jump through. This is a way of digging reservoirs in the desert that they will drink from later. What might sometimes look like arcane, arid academic learning might actually be teaching us disciplines that will become very important for pastoral ministry later. We need to resist the cultural demand that everything pay off *right now*. Scholarly reflection just doesn't work that way.

Even when I'm doing higher-level scholarship in peer-reviewed journals, I ultimately hope that there's an investment in the community that shows its worth later on. The point is not, "We'll be smart Christians. Other people won't think we're naïve or dummies." The point is that it will make us a better community of practice.

The point where pragmatism makes intuitive sense is the tension of Jesus's priorities: pastoring people, caring for the poor, and so on. Intellectual reflection requires time and energy. At times, the two seem to be in opposition.

CM: In *Desiring the Kingdom*, you talk about the best account of human beings being driven by love. You then spend a lot of time reflecting on this idea that human beings are formed by things that draw their love out. Could you explain how you've been thinking about formation and the way that church practices play into that?

JKAS: To make the core claim that human beings are lovers and that we're defined by what we love is really only the beginning of this package. Then the question is, How do I come to love what I love?

The tradition and work I've drawn upon emphasizes that your love is much more like a habit than a decision. It is a fundamental orientation that you acquire, but it is a product of a process that philosophers call "habituation." That is, you are trained to love. It's a bit complicated for charismatics, but it's not the case that there is just some magic event that stimulates love to the right track and then you're all set. I think we all know this just doesn't work.

Your heart is the fulcrum of your love, and the heart is subject to training and to formation. The way our hearts get trained is through immersion in practices, rituals and routines and rhythms that, over time, inscribe the right disposition within us. These practices orient us so that we are becoming the kind of people trained to the goal of loving well.

It doesn't have to be mystifying. It's similar to how we learn to play the violin or to drive. Historically these practices are called spiritual disciplines; they habituate our love over time so that we become those kinds of people.

CM: Now, is this similar to what someone like Dallas Willard would say about the spiritual disciplines and formation of the heart?

JKAS: Absolutely; there are tons of overlap. The difference that I try to amplify in *Desiring the Kingdom* is that Dallas still tends to paint a picture of spiritual disciplines that maybe doesn't have quite the centrality of gathered Christian worship about it. My emphasis is on the practice of gathered Christian worship as the hub for that formation. All of our other spiritual disciplines spiral out of that hub and live off the energy and formative power of the centrality of the church. You need the church to pull off spiritual discipline.

CM: What is it about the church in particular that makes it the hub of formation? Why do you think the church is so important?

JKAS: I'm not sure to what extent the Vineyard will go with me, but I'll say this. One, I think that gathered Christian worship is the hot spot of the Spirit; I think it should be sacramental. By that, I mean the Spirit is most powerfully present in what we receive as the sacraments and in what the church over time has discerned as core worship practices.

So if you want to be formed by the Spirit and sanctified by what the church over history has said, then you immerse yourself in these practices: the Lord's Supper, the Word, and baptism. One of the reasons ecclesial worship is essential is its sacramental character.

Secondly, for me, the core of the practices of Christian worship are catholic—not that they are Roman Catholic, but that they are the common inheritance of the people of God, over history, led by the Spirit. In that process, the church together has discerned a kind of form or shape of Christian worship that the Spirit works in.

The entire narrative of what God is doing through Christ is re-narrated every week in catholic Christian worship practices. So catholicity, to me, simply means inheriting a core commitment to certain components of Christian worship that have their own logic about them. They are liturgies. They tell the story of the gospel over and over. In doing that, they initiate us into the story.

What worries me is that if you don't appreciate that catholic heritage of worship, you lose components of the story. Then you lose certain opportunities for formation and counterformation to the secular liturgies we are immersed in.

CM: So you're saying that, as humans, we are always being formed in one direction or another, and the church provides a crucial location for Christian formation over against other dominant sources of formation in culture. In the book, you talk about the "liturgy of the stadium" and compare that with what's happening in the church. Could you unpack that a bit?

JKAS: I take the "liturgy of the stadium" to represent American civil religion. The entire book of Revelation is God's critique of the liturgies of the empire and how Christian worship is counter to that. (By the way, you can't underestimate the function of the principalities and powers in these other liturgies, the rival liturgies.)

The claim that Christian worship is counterformative to the formation of the liturgy of American civil religion only works if you have received the intentionality of the shape of historic Christian worship. If you've mistakenly thought that you can take the content of Christianity and drop it into any old form you want, and if you've said, "Well, in the name of being relevant and accessible, we're just going to do worship like the mall or like the concert or the stadium," then, I'm sorry, but you don't have any counterformative possibilities. You've just lost the logic of the practice. Instead you just have this pastiche thing. You've distilled Jesus into this content that you can drop into any old form you want. But the fact remains that the form itself is already a liturgical formation. If you Jesu-fy the mall, you've just commodified Jesus. I think that many so-called seeker-sensitive strategies misstep on this point.

CM: Is that part of what you were saying earlier about how you felt there's a strong connection between this way of thinking about love and formation and evangelism?

JKAS: In some sense. As Saint Augustine says in the opening of the *Confessions*, his spiritual autobiography: "You have made us for yourself, and our hearts are restless until they rest in thee."

He doesn't say we're looking for answers or knowledge. He says we're looking for a home for our restless hearts and our wandering loves. The *Confessions* is a long documentary of someone looking for love in all the wrong places.

Too much of our evangelism has been informed by picturing human beings as "thinking things." So when someone sees that bumper sticker, "Jesus is the answer," they might think, But what's the question? But if you look at it from Augustine's paradigm of the human being as lover, people aren't looking for answers to questions. They're not looking to solve an intellectual puzzle. They want to love. They're looking *for* love, and they're looking *to* love. What we bring to them is the Lover of their souls who alone can satisfy that longing.

But this means that you must recognize and build on the fact that so many things people do in contemporary culture is a manifestation of their longing, of their desire. Christianity is not fundamentally the answer to a set of intellectual questions that people have; Christianity is the love story that finally lets people make sense of their desire.

I think grasping that truth would change how we do evangelism, missions, outreach, even in deeply secularized contexts, where people aren't asking religious questions at all—but they are engaged in all kinds of practices of desire and longing and love.

CM: Let's return to the question of beliefs for a moment—I want to raise a flag for the importance of articulate belief. To what extent does the content of propositional belief begin to play a role in that experience of having one's desire fulfilled? Because as you go on the journey, it seems like the content of belief becomes more and more important to informing the journey.

JKAS: I think so too. But why did the church begin formulating creeds and confessions in the first place? Because we needed to find out who the Jesus we were praying to actually was. We were searching for the nature of the triune God we pray to.

The articulation of the content is clarifying who we worship and who we long for. That's important to keep track of, so you don't end up effectively putting an idol in its place. The articulation of Christian truth, the preaching of the Word, and the articulation of the Scriptures are always making us sure we know who we love.

What you can get in "secular society" is a kind of back-handed affirmation of some of our disordered loves too. So when you see a culture that is riven with consumerism, you realize they're looking for something. I wonder what it looks like for evangelism and mission and outreach to almost honor or recognize that this is the manifestation of love; of disordered love. Like G. K. Chesterton reportedly said, "Any man knocking on a brothel is secretly looking for God."

CM: So from this perspective, you could say that the pursuit of right belief is essentially an assault on idolatry—but it has to be understood in the context of a community of love or else itself become an idol.

JKAS: Exactly.

CM: So we've talked a lot about spiritual formation and communal liturgical practices. But Protestants, in particular, pay a great deal of attention to preaching—especially preaching the Bible in an expository way. I know that's something you appreciate too. But how might this sort of shift in thinking about practices potentially affect the way that a church planter thinks about preaching?

JKAS: None of this diminishes the importance of preaching, but I do think it recalibrates how we think of preaching. From this perspective, preaching is not primarily the dissemination of information. Instead it is the storytelling of the narrative of what God is doing in Christ to redeem the world. It should be something that is more like poetry than discourse.

There is something irreducible about a story. It's not a mistake that historically the church has been narrating one huge story. Here's where N. T. Wright's model for seeing the drama of Scripture in its multiple acts just becomes a new frame and context for seeing how our preaching of the Word invites people into the drama. It is a story that effectively pulls us into what God is doing.

There's a great book by a friend of mine. It's some years old now, but it's by John Wright, named *Telling God's Story*. I believe it is a brilliant introduction to reconfiguring preaching as "Here is what it looks like to preach in a way that communicates to people on a heart level. It communicates to their imaginations." I think good preaching is not so much about filling the intellect as it is about recruiting the imagination. Wright's book is an excellent resource to prime people to think about that.

CM: And in a lot of ways, having that narrative perspective can heighten the sense of significance around what churches do, day in and day out. It underlines the holiness and profundity of the very existence of your little church plant in Whatevertown, USA. You're not just trying to succeed; you're trying to participate in the mission of God from the beginning to the end.

JKAS: That's right. One little congregation is as much a stage for that drama as any other.

CM: That's probably something that anyone who has planted a church will know they need to hear more than once, because you're going to get the kitchen sink thrown at you from day one. Knowing that you're in a story of immense cosmic significance makes all the difference in the world.

JKAS: This is another one of those places where I think the Vineyard has indigenous intuitions along this line. Anecdotally, my impression is that a lot of Vineyard churches have always tried to make room for the arts. They understand the kind of aesthetic register on which God can get ahold of us. So, in a way, this is about trying to think of the entirety of worship on that aesthetic register, not just so it's pretty or aesthetic, but because we are aesthetic kinds of animals, and that's how God gets ahold of us. It's not like we move from worship, which is singing, and then we move to preaching, which is information. Instead, all of this is a piece of an aesthetic affective mode by which God is getting ahold of us.

CM: I think especially in churches like the Vineyard, where we pay attention to things like prayer ministry, there's a trajectory in which the hope that the imagination is being opened to God "getting ahold of us" leads directly to a hope for an encounter with God's living presence. Something like that changes the equation profoundly! Coming out of a pentecostal background, this is probably familiar to you— where the hope is that all the ideas and the practices and the preaching are lit on fire by the real presence of God. In that sense, the whole thing becomes sacramental in the best of all possible worlds.

OK, to stay on this topic but pivot slightly, in the Roman Catholic tradition (among others) people take very seriously the wisdom of the church over time—it has for them a kind of authority that Protestants know not of. In your position, with a foot in the pentecostal world and a foot in the more historic forms of the classical traditions of the church, do you have suggestions for ways that less "liturgically informed" churches can meaningfully connect to a catholic tradition without, say, having to become Roman Catholic or Orthodox or Anglican to own it?

JKAS: I think so. Part of that step is just not being intimidated by Roman Catholics or Anglicans who might give the impression that this heritage is their own possession. It's not. It is the common inheritance of Christians. Modernity encouraged us to forget that, and we bear some blame for it. That is what Charles Taylor calls the trajectory of "excarnation" that characterized Protestantism. Other church movements can do this authentically in ways which are true to their own DNA strands.

Here's an analogy. My pentecostal friends who appreciate these points and are trying to remember catholicity in worship can tell themselves the story "You know, we really kind of grew out of the Wesleyan tradition." John Wesley headed a renewal movement within Anglican Christianity. In fact, a lot of what he wanted to do was to revivify and enliven what looks to us now like pretty historic Christian practices. So Pentecostals can find ways internal to their own traditions to reconnect themselves to those roots without feeling that it is inauthentic.

For the Vineyard or other traditions to go about narrating that story, it's very important that you look for resources, signals, triggers and hooks internal to your sort of "indigenous spirituality" that you can leverage. You're Christians.

You didn't fall from the sky. Your traditions came out of a heritage. There's some indebtedness in there somewhere. So look for those hooks. Because, otherwise, the worst thing that could happen is what I call "liturgical chic," where people say, "These candles and stuff are really cool. Let's try this out." But that doesn't get the logic of the practice.

CM: You raise a helpful point when you talk about simply not being intimidated. But inquiring into these older ways while being rooted in the knowledge that God has called this movement to exist for a purpose gives a great deal of freedom to explore. Then you're building on something that's already good, as opposed to making up for a gap where Protestants think they might be falling short.

JKAS: Right. The injunction to articulate your catholicity is not saying, "Well, I should just go be Anglican." It's realizing your own accent on that catholicity, the Spirit-led improvisation that the Vineyard brings to the whole body of Christ.

CM: Getting very practical now, in the Vineyard there are an increasing number of practitioners, pastors, and church planters who are also becoming interested in the life of the mind. But for many of those people, the journey might not necessarily include going to seminary or getting a PhD. So what are the most important resources that busy, pragmatic, often bivocational church planters might need to pursue the flourishing life of their minds?

JKAS: I feel a little inadequate to answer, only because it seems that the answer might be relevant just to a particular cross section or context. But let's start with this. One of the things that people who are able to pursue more dedicated reflection should do is find ways to translate, collect, and disseminate what they think are important reflection resources for the "busy church planter." These people should recommend them regularly to others.

Some of it is essentially the mundane stuff of developing really good reading habits. But peer communities and scholars working to suggest resources would be good for reflection as well. They could identify reflective practices to carry out once a month or once a quarter. Discern the moment and see what is relevant.

The Christian scholar needs to be an amphibious creature who has enough of a foot in academia that she has ears to hear and is attentive to the shifts. But she also has a foot in the community of practice so that she knows where the questions are pushing, what people need to be thinking about.

CM: And for those who do pursue further intellectual training, could you reflect on the significance of regular church life for Christian scholars?

JKAS: The local church is the space of gathered worship and shared pursuit of the spiritual disciplines. I believe gathered congregational worship is still the central incubation space for our imagination. So if I'm going to be a Christian scholar, there is no way my intuitions and sensibilities and interests and concerns are going to be functionally and effectively Christian if I'm not regularly immersed in the practices of the people of God, with the people of God. I might have all the great Christian theories and ideas and perspectives, but I need to be part of that people.

The other reason is, there are just such crucial virtues that will be formed in me by being part of that local congregation. I'm going to have to learn patience, humility, compassion, and forgiveness. Learning humility is especially important for people who have scholarly predilections.

And thirdly, we must follow what Cardinal Newman called "the sense of the faithful." At the end of the day, I see the plumber down the pew who is wiser than I am. I don't care how many degrees I have; he is wiser than I am. He's actually a better follower of Jesus than I am. If I fall into the intellectualist trap that people who think the most are the most faithful, I'm doomed. So I need to stay in spaces where I'm disciplined in that regard.

CM: Asking the question in that direction, are there specific ways from your life experience that you can suggest or imagine ways for churches—individually and at a movement level—to most effectively make space for nascent scholars in their midst?

JKAS: I've seen ways in which it does and doesn't work. I can think of two churches. One was a church plant we were a part of, and the pastors and leaders of that community had a strong enough sense of their mission and calling and identity in the Lord that my presence there as a scholar was received by them as a gift. I was like the theologian in residence for that church plant in Philadelphia, and it was fantastic. But you need the sort of leaders who are comfortable and confident enough in themselves to be able to do that.

And I was in another congregation where, even when I turned on the humility full tilt, some of its leaders felt threatened in the presence of a scholar. Looking back, I do think it was because of their own insecurities.

Now, that doesn't turn into a strict formula, but it's something to watch for. Scholars need to do a very good job of affirming the callings of congregations and what they're doing, to signal that they're there to serve. And then congregations need to find ways to receive scholars as gifts that God brings to them.

PHILOSOPHY, CULTURE, AND COMMUNICATION

An Interview

Kenneth Sheppard: You're currently teaching philosophy at Calvin College, and you've written a series of books, from academic philosophical studies to collections of op-ed essays about contemporary Christianity. For *Patrol* readers who aren't familiar with your work, tell us a little about your journey: when you became a Christian, when and why you decided upon a life in academia.

James K. A. Smith: I wasn't raised in the church and became a Christian when I was eighteen years old, back in Canada (through my girlfriend—now wife—doing a little missionary dating). This was a sort of Damascus Road experience for me, not because I'd been a licentious frat boy

This interview originally appeared in *Patrol: A Review of Religion and the Modern World* (October 2010) at www.patrolmag.com. Reprinted with permission.

but because I quickly discovered why I had a brain. I immediately abandoned my plans to become an architect in order to pursue what I sensed was a call to pastoral ministry. When I was a sophomore in college, I discovered Reformed theology and then, shortly afterward, began reading Francis Schaeffer and, later, Alvin Plantinga. All sorts of lights went on for me and I began to sense that perhaps my calling was to be a Christian scholar.

So at the end of college, I had to choose between seminary and grad school in philosophy. It was a real struggle for me—one of the few really existential *choices* I had to make. But when we settled on the academic direction, everything sort of fell into place, and I was at peace with the decision. I'm sometimes still tempted by pastoral ministry a bit, but it's a heck of a lot more work, so that usually passes pretty quickly.

However, I do think it's been that sort of "pastoral" side that has always made me inclined to be a scholar who tries to serve the church—trying to think through issues and challenges in order to help the church be a faithful witness in our late modern culture. I think that's what's behind my more "popular" work: I sometimes describe that as "outreach scholarship." My exemplar here is Rich Mouw, one of my predecessors in the philosophy department at Calvin and now president of Fuller Seminary. Rich is the model of what we might call an "ecclesial scholar."

KS: Part of your own story has been a navigation between philosophy and theology, between Pentecostalism and Reformed Calvinism, and between Christianity and contemporary Western culture. What has drawn you in these different directions? You edit a book series, and you're completing a series of volumes [the three-volume *Cultural Liturgies* project] that seems to navigate these issues more concretely. What are you hoping to accomplish? Where do you see yourself moving in the future?

JKAS: When you put it this way, I just sound like a kind of theological mutt! There's a pilgrimage that can be plotted in my trajectory from dispensationalism through Pentecostalism and into the Reformed tradition, but I won't bore you with that here. (In *Letters to a Young Calvinist*, I talk about this as a path to becoming catholic, oddly enough.) I think the Pentecostal and Reformed streams come together in my new book, *Thinking in Tongues: Pentecostal Contributions to Christian Philosophy*. Anyway, these are features of autobiography more than some intentional "choice."

As for the diverse projects and what I'm hoping to accomplish—that's an interesting question. I guess I'm working on multiple fronts. A lot of my work has been on postmodernism (including my editing of the "Church and Postmodern Culture" book series). This is where I'm trying to take my expertise in European philosophy and use it to help Christians understand cultural shifts and the impact of ideas on contemporary culture—again, with the goal of thinking carefully about the shape of Christian practice.

It was this that gave rise to my "Cultural Liturgies" trilogy, of which *Desiring the Kingdom* is the first volume. In a way, I can plot the trajectory to this project from chapter 7 of my earlier book, *Introducing Radical Orthodoxy*, and the chapter on Foucault in *Who's Afraid of Postmodernism?* In general, I think Christians have operated with a reductionistic notion of culture—reducing it to the level of ideas—and failed to appreciate the affective dynamics of cultural formation. That can be both detrimental and a missed opportunity. It's also part of why Protestants—and evangelicals in particular—have been largely unreflective about the formative role of worship. So the second volume, *Imagining the Kingdom: How Worship Works*, is going to explore what I'm calling the "mechanics" of liturgical formation by exploring an analogy between literature and liturgy, drawing on research at the intersection of literature and cognitive science. The third volume will focus on politics: the wager there is that thinking about politics in terms of liturgy changes the debate. In doing so, I ultimately hope to respond to Jeffrey Stout's critique of what he calls the "new traditionalism" (Hauerwas, MacIntyre, Milbank) in his very important book, *Democracy and Tradition*.

Alas, I'm rambling. I won't bore you with all my projects. What am I trying to accomplish? Well, on the one hand, you could say that I'm regularly trying to get evangelicals to remember they are catholic. That is, I'm trying to press evangelicals to see themselves as connected to the catholic heritage of Christian faith and practice. On the other hand, I'm hoping to help Christians understand the dynamics of contemporary culture—to appreciate, celebrate, mine, and criticize contemporary culture as both an expression of humanity's culture-making mandate while also recognizing how disordered cultural institutions can be. My hero in this respect is Saint Augustine, and his *City of God* is doing something similar, I think, in a different cultural context.

So yeah: that's sort of my goal. And of course, I'd like to be mildly famous. Any Christian scholar or public intellectual who doesn't own up to that sinful desire has obviously not read Augustine's *Confessions*, especially book 10. There Augustine gives a great, almost psychoanalytic analysis of the tensions we experience: when we try to do what's right and good, we end up getting praise, and then we can easily fall into the trap of doing this stuff *in order to* get fame and praise. I'm enough of a Calvinist to be constantly aware of this. In fact, doing interviews really fuels such vainglory. Maybe we should stop right here.

KS: Given both your academic and more popular work, what has drawn you to write for both audiences? How does a Christian academic trained in Continental philosophy attempt to contribute to contemporary discussions of Christianity in both a critical but accessible way? Is there anything about the nature of this commitment that you see embedded within Christian belief and practice itself?

JKAS: Well, I don't want to imply that all Christian scholars *have* to write for more popular audiences. It is of course a legitimate calling to simply speak into the conversations in a specialized discipline, and I don't want to diminish the importance of that sort of "witness" as a Christian scholar. Plus, writing for wider audiences isn't always easy and certainly isn't automatic. The guilds of scholarship don't often train us to communicate in ways that are widely accessible: instead they tend to inculcate us into specialist jargon that we use as a shorthand with the other six people in our subdiscipline. So some scholars just won't have the skills or gifts to be able to speak to wider audiences. And that's OK.

On the other hand, I do think Christian scholars have a

special sort of obligation to the church as a "public." I think we owe debts to our Christian brothers and sisters, and that the life of the church often buoys our imagination more than we realize. I know I've always had a sense that I'm able to do what I do because of Christian communities and constituencies that make it possible for me to be a scholar and a teacher. So I think I owe something to them, and the best way to love my brothers and sisters is for me to share my gifts with them—which, in my case, means trying to find ways to share the fruits of my scholarship.

KS: There seems to be a reinvigorated debate among Christians about how they should understand and engage the culture in which they live. You have written a review of James Davison Hunter's book *To Change the World* [see chapter 8 above], and you've interviewed Hunter himself. Perhaps you'd like to be a bit more explicit about what you see as at stake in these debates? Although it's a complex subject, how would you suggest Christians today might better understand and engage their cultural context?

JKAS: I think we're in a time of some ferment about Christianity and culture right now, especially among evangelicals. Granted, you still have the kind of "relevance" phenomenon—post-fundamentalist evangelicals who are geeked to learn that they might be able to listen to Coldplay and go to R-rated movies and thus tend to just have a naïve enthusiasm about cultural engagement in the name of being "relevant." I tire of that really quickly and have to work hard not to be condescending.

But there is another interesting development afoot. I

think something like a watered-down, distorted Kuyperian project has taken hold of evangelicalism over the last generation (think of Chuck Colson's book, *How Now Shall We Live?*, which was kind of a Schaefferian Kuyper for evangelicals). This sort of woke evangelicals from their acultural slumbers, but it really only woke them *to* partisan federal politics and, as such, underwrote the rise of the Religious Right. And the big problem with the Religious Right is the instrumentalization of Christianity for the sake of American civil religion. In other words, the real danger is confusing faith in God for faith in America.

Now there's a generation of people who are entirely disenchanted with this confusion and conflation, but they're expressing that in very different ways. You have the sort of Shane Claiborne / Greg Boyd vaguely "Anabaptist" response on the one hand, but then also a renewal of two-kingdoms thinking among the young, restless, and Reformed crowd. Both share concerns about the shape of American civil religion, I think, but have different prescriptions.

Hunter's book drops into this ferment. I think it's a very important book, hopefully displacing the tired, overblown influence of Niebuhr's *Christ and Culture*. Hunter diagnoses this situation with a more sophisticated understanding of culture and cultural change. And what I think is most significant is the extent to which he is sympathetic to the neo-Anabaptist project, as he calls it. Of course he's ultimately critical of it, but I think he appreciates it more than most mainstream commentators. Indeed, I think his prescription for "faithful presence" in the elite spaces of culture-shaping institutions is closer to the Anabaptist vision than he sometimes realizes.

I hope my work, especially *Desiring the Kingdom*, sort of supplements his analysis by also helping us to appreciate the formative power of cultural practices. Indeed, I describe them as "secular liturgies," and I think analyzing culture through the lens of worship raises the stakes. And again, I think this is exactly the sort of analysis Augustine was undertaking in *City of God*: the empire was not just a political reality—it was informed by disordered *worship*. I think we need a similar "liturgical" analysis of culture.

CPSIA information can be obtained at www.ICGtesting.com
Printed in the USA
LVOW10s0405140814

398848LV00001B/12/P

9 781937 555085